KETO CHAFFLE RECIPES

Delicious Ketogenic Low Carb Chaffle Recipes
to Reverse Diabetes and Turn Your Body into a
Fat Burning Machine

Isabella Karent

TABLE OF CONTENTS

INTRODUCTION

The almighty keto diet is indeed a game changer in the "weight loss" world. I am always amazed and excited anytime I open my social media pages and I see "before" and "after" pictures of people who are following a well-planned keto diet. Sometimes, I ask myself "Is this diet that effective?" Yes, the keto diet is very effective. The diet has a way of turning your body into a fat burning machine.

When you are following a keto diet, your body will be starved of glucose because you are not consuming enough carbohydrate foods. Consequently, your body will have to look for another way of generating energy. The next option for your body is fat. Your liver will start converting the fat in your body into ketones. The ketones are what will be used to power all body cells and fuel metabolism. When this is achieved, your body is in ketosis. In this manner, your body will be burning your body fat as energy and you will start losing weight, even while you are sleeping.

The increased interest in the keto diet overtime has ushered in a lot of creativity in the culinary world. A lot of substitute for high carb meals have emerged. One of those great high carb meal substitutes is the chaffle. A chaffle is a keto friendly form of waffles that is made with egg and cheese. Chaffles are very delicious and they are very easy to make.

A lot of the "keto people" have fallen in love with chaffles. However, eating chaffles may become boring and monotonous at times if you do not have different chaffle recipes at hand. This cookbook is written to provide more delicious and easier chaffle recipes to "keto people" who love chaffles. This cookbook is packed with 50 finger-licking recipes that can turn your body into a fat burning machine. Enjoy!!!

CAULIFLOWER CHAFFLE

PREP TIME: 5 minutes

COOK TIME: 8 minutes

SERVINGS: 2

Ingredients:

- 1 cup cauliflower rice
- ¼ tsp salt or to taste
- 1 tbsp melted butter
- 1 egg
- ¼ tsp nutmeg
- ¼ tsp cinnamon
- ¼ tsp garlic powder
- 1/8 tsp ground black pepper or to taste
- 1/8 tsp white pepper or to taste
- ¼ tsp Italian seasoning
- ½ cup shredded parmesan cheese
- ½ cup shredded mozzarella cheese

Garnish:

- Chopped green onions

Directions:

1. Pour ¼ of the parmesan cheese into a blender, add the mozzarella cheese, egg, salt, nutmeg, butter,

cinnamon, garlic powder, black pepper, white pepper, Italian seasoning and cauliflower.

2. Add the egg and blend until you form a smooth batter.
3. Plug the waffle maker and preheat it. Spray the waffle maker with a non-stick spray.
4. Sprinkle about tbsp of the remaining parmesan cheese on top of the waffle maker.
5. Fill the waffle maker with ¼ of the batter and spread out the batter to cover all the holes on the waffle maker. Sprinkle some shredded parmesan over the batter.
6. Close the lid of the waffle maker and cook for about 4 to 5 minutes or according to your waffle maker's settings.
7. After the cooking cycle, remove the waffle with a rubber or silicone utensil.
8. Repeat step 4 to 7 until you have cooked all the batter into chaffles.
9. Serve and enjoy.

Nutrition Facts
Servings: 2

Amount per serving	
Calories	220
% Daily Value*	
Total Fat 15.8g	20%
Saturated Fat 9.1g	46%
Cholesterol 119mg	40%

Nutrition Facts

Servings: 2

Sodium 698mg	30%
Total Carbohydrate 6.2g	2%
Dietary Fiber 0.6g	2%
Total Sugars 2.4g	
Protein 15g	
Vitamin D 12mcg	58%
Calcium 249mg	19%
Iron 1mg	4%
Potassium 40mg	1%

KETO PUMPKIN CHAFFLE

PREP TIME: 5 minutes

COOK TIME: 16 minutes

SERVINGS: 2

Ingredients:

- 1 cup finely shredded mozzarella cheese
- 2 tsp pumpkin pie spice
- ½ tsp ground ginger
- ¼ cup pumpkin puree
- ½ tsp vanilla extract
- 2 large eggs
- 1 tbsp almond flour
- ½ tsp baking powder
- 2 tsp sugar free maple syrup

Directions:

1. Plug the waffle maker and preheat it. Spray it with non-stick spray.
2. In a large mixing bowl, combine the baking powder, almond flour, ginger, and pumpkin.
3. Add the eggs, vanilla extract, maple syrup, cheese and pumpkin puree. Mix until the ingredients are well combined and you have formed a smooth batter.

4. Fill the waffle iron with ¼ of the batter and spread out the batter to cover all the holes on the waffle maker.

5. Close the lid of the waffle maker and cook for about 3 to 4 minutes or according to your waffle maker's settings.

6. After the cooking cycle, remove the chaffle from the iron and set aside.

7. Repeat step 4 to 6 until you have cooked all the batter into chaffles.

8. Serve and enjoy.

Nutrition Facts	
Servings: 2	
Amount per serving	
Calories	**216**
% Daily Value*	
Total Fat 14.8g	19%
Saturated Fat 3.7g	19%
Cholesterol 194mg	65%
Sodium 166mg	7%
Total Carbohydrate 9.3g	3%
Dietary Fiber 2.7g	10%
Total Sugars 2.2g	
Protein 13.8g	
Vitamin D 18mcg	88%
Calcium 141mg	11%
Iron 2mg	13%
Potassium 275mg	6%

KETO CHOCOLATE CHAFFLES

PREP TIME: 5 minutes

COOK TIME: 8 minutes

SERVINGS: 2

Ingredients:

- 1 tsp swerve
- 1 large egg
- 2 tbsp cream cheese
- 1 tbsp unsweetened cocoa powder
- 2 tbsp almond flour
- 1/4 tsp baking powder
- 1 tsp vanilla extract

Topping:

- 1 tbsp granulated swerve
- ¼ tsp vanilla extract
- ¼ tsp cinnamon
- 2 tbsp cream cheese (softened)

Directions:

1. Plug the waffle maker and preheat it. Spray it with non-stick spray.
2. In a large mixing bowl, combine the almond flour, stevia extract, baking powder and cocoa powder.

3. Add the eggs, cream cheese and vanilla extract. Mix until the ingredients are well combined and you have formed a smooth batter.

4. Fill the waffle maker with the batter. Spread out the batter to cover all the holes on the waffle maker.

5. Close the lid of the waffle maker and bake for about 4 minutes or until the chaffle is crispy.

6. After the cooking cycle, remove the chaffle from the iron using a plastic or silicone utensil and set aside.

7. Repeat step 4 to 5 until you have cooked all the batter into waffles.

8. Leave the batter to cool completely.

9. Meanwhile, prepare the topping. Combine the cream cheese, vanilla extract, cinnamon and swerve in a mixing bowl and mix until smooth.

10. Top chaffles with the cream cheese mixture and enjoy.

Nutrition Facts	
Servings: 2	
Amount per serving	
Calories	283
% Daily Value*	
Total Fat 23.8g	31%
Saturated Fat 6.4g	32%
Cholesterol 115mg	38%
Sodium 106mg	5%
Total Carbohydrate 10.1g	4%
Dietary Fiber 4.1g	14%
Total Sugars 1.6g	

Nutrition Facts	
Servings: 2	
Protein 11.2g	
Vitamin D 9mcg	44%
Calcium 123mg	9%
Iron 2mg	12%
Potassium 167mg	4%

ZUCCHINI BACON CHAFFLES

PREP TIME: 10 minutes

COOK TIME: 12 minutes

SERVINGS: 2

Ingredients:

- 1 cup grated zucchini
- 1 tbsp bacon bits (finely chopped)
- ¼ cup shredded mozzarella cheese
- ½ cup shredded parmesan
- ½ tsp salt or to taste
- ½ tsp ground black pepper or to taste
- ½ tsp onion powder
- ¼ tsp nutmeg
- 2 eggs

Directions:

1. Add ¼ tsp salt to the grated zucchini and let it sit for about 5 minutes.
2. Put the grated zucchini in a clean towel and squeeze out excess water.
3. Plug the waffle maker and preheat it. Spray it with non-stick spray.
4. Break the eggs into a mixing bowl and beat.

5. Add the grated zucchini, bacon bit, nutmeg, onion powder, pepper, salt and mozzarella.

6. Add ¾ of the parmesan cheese. You have to set aside some parmesan cheese.

7. Mix until the ingredients are well combined.

8. Fill the preheated waffle maker with the batter and spread out the batter to the edge to cover all the holes on the waffle maker.

9. Close the waffle maker lid and cook until the chaffle is golden brown and crispy. The zucchini chaffle may take longer than other chaffles to get crispy.

10. After the baking cycle, use a plastic or silicone utensil to remove the chaffle from the waffle maker.

11. Repeat step 8 to 10 until you have cooked all the batter into chaffles.

12. Serve and enjoy.

Nutrition Facts	
Servings: 2	
Amount per serving	
Calories	**216**
% Daily Value*	
Total Fat 13.6g	17%
Saturated Fat 5.4g	27%
Cholesterol 183mg	61%
Sodium 903mg	39%
Total Carbohydrate 4.7g	2%
Dietary Fiber 0.9g	3%

Nutrition Facts

Servings: 2

Total Sugars 1.6g

Protein 20.4g

Vitamin D 15mcg	77%
Calcium 263mg	20%
Iron 1mg	7%
Potassium 220mg	5%

APPLE PIE CHAFFLE

PREP TIME: 10 minutes

COOK TIME: 6 minutes

SERVINGS: 2

Ingredients:

- 1 egg (beaten)
- 1 tbsp almond flour
- 1 big apple (finely chopped)
- 1 tbsp heavy whipping cream
- 1 tsp cinnamon
- 1 tbsp granulated swerve
- ½ tsp vanilla extract
- 1/3 cup mozzarella cheese

Topping:

- ¼ tbsp sugar free maple syrup

Directions:

1. Plug the waffle maker and preheat it. Spray it with non-stick spray.
2. In a large mixing bowl, combine the swerve, almond flour, mozzarella, cinnamon and chopped apple.
3. Add the eggs, vanilla extract and heavy whipping cream. Mix until all the ingredients are well combined.

4. Fill the waffle maker with the batter and spread out the batter to the edges of the waffle maker to all the holes on it.

5. Close the lid of the waffle maker and cook for about 4 minute or according to waffle maker's settings.

6. After the cooking cycle, remove the chaffle from the waffle maker with a plastic or silicone utensil.

7. Repeat step 4 to 6 until you have cooked all the batter into chaffles.

8. Serve and top with maple syrup.

Nutrition Facts	
Servings: 2	
Amount per serving	
Calories	**158**
% Daily Value*	
Total Fat 7.8g	10%
Saturated Fat 3g	15%
Cholesterol 95mg	32%
Sodium 64mg	3%
Total Carbohydrate 19g	7%
Dietary Fiber 3.7g	13%
Total Sugars 12.1g	
Protein 5.4g	
Vitamin D 12mcg	58%
Calcium 40mg	3%
Iron 1mg	6%

Nutrition Facts	
Servings: 2	
Potassium 161mg	3%

BUFFALO CHICKEN CHAFFLE

PREP TIME: 10 minutes

COOK TIME: 10 minutes

SERVINGS: 2

Ingredients:

- 1 egg
- 5 ounces cooked chicken (diced)
- 2 tbsp buffalo sauce
- ½ tsp garlic powder
- ½ tsp onion powder
- ½ tsp dried basil
- 5 tbsp shredded cheddar cheese
- 2 ounces cream cheese

Directions:

1. Plug the waffle maker and preheat it. Spray it with non-stick spray.
2. In a large mixing bowl, combine the onion powder, basil, garlic, buffalo sauce, cheddar cheese chicken and cream cheese. Mix until the ingredients are well combined and you have formed a smooth batter.
3. Sprinkle some shredded cheddar cheese over the waffle maker and pour in adequate amount of the batter. Spread

out the batter to the edges of the waffle maker to cover al the holes on the waffle maker.

4. Close the lid of the waffle maker and cook for about 3 to 4 minutes or according to waffle maker's settings.

5. After the cooking cycle, remove the chaffle from the waffle maker with a plastic or silicone utensil.

6. Repeat step 3 to 5 until you have cooked all the batter into chaffles.

7. Serve and enjoy.

Nutrition Facts
Servings: 2

Amount per serving	
Calories	313
% Daily Value*	
Total Fat 20.1g	26%
Saturated Fat 11.2g	56%
Cholesterol 186mg	62%
Sodium 270mg	12%
Total Carbohydrate 2.2g	1%
Dietary Fiber 0.1g	0%
Total Sugars 0.7g	
Protein 30g	
Vitamin D 10mcg	49%
Calcium 174mg	13%
Iron 2mg	9%
Potassium 227mg	5%

CHOCO PEANUT BUTTER CHAFFLE

PREP TIME: 5 minutes

COOK TIME: 10 minutes

SERVINGS: 2

Ingredients:

Filling:

- 3 tbsp all-natural peanut butter
- 2 tsp swerve sweetener
- 1 tsp vanilla extract
- 2 tbsp heavy cream

Chaffle:

- ¼ tsp baking powder
- 1 tbsp unsweetened cocoa powder
- 4 tsp almond flour
- ½ tsp vanilla extract
- 1 tbsp granulated swerve sweetener
- 1 large egg (beaten)
- 1 tbsp heavy cream

Directions:

For the chaffle:

1. Plug the waffle maker and preheat it. Spray it with a non-stick spray.

2. In a large mixing bowl, combine the almond flour, cocoa powder, baking powder and swerve.

3. Add the egg, vanilla extract and heavy cream. Mix until the ingredients are well combined and you form a smooth batter.

4. Pour some of the batter into the preheated waffle maker. Spread out the batter to the edges of the waffle maker to cover all the holes on the waffle iron.

5. Close the lid of the waffle iron and bake for about 5 minutes or according to waffle maker's settings.

6. After the baking cycle, use a plastic or silicone utensil to remove the chaffle from the waffle maker.

7. Repeat step 4 to 6 until you have cooked all the batter into chaffles.

8. Transfer the chaffles to a wire rack and let the chaffles cool completely.

9. **For the filling:**

10. Combine the vanilla, swerve, heavy cream and peanut butter in a bowl. Mix until the ingredients are well combined.

11. Spread the peanut butter frosting over the chaffles and serve.

12. Enjoy.

Nutrition Facts	
Servings: 2	
Amount per serving	
Calories	560
% Daily Value*	

Nutrition Facts

Servings: 2

Total Fat 43.2g	55%
Saturated Fat 8.8g	44%
Cholesterol 124mg	41%
Sodium 168mg	7%
Total Carbohydrate 32g	12%
Dietary Fiber 8.1g	29%
Total Sugars 9g	
Protein 19g	
Vitamin D 20mcg	102%
Calcium 179mg	14%
Iron 3mg	19%
Potassium 160mg	3%

SLOPPY JOE CHAFFLE

PREP TIME: 10 minutes

COOK TIME: 20 minutes

SERVINGS: 2

Ingredients:

Chaffle:

- 1 large egg (beaten)
- 1/8 tsp onion powder
- 1 tbsp almond flour
- ½ cup shredded mozzarella cheese
- 1 tsp nutmeg
- ¼ tsp baking powder

Sloppy Joe Filling:

- 2 tsp olive oil
- 1 pounds ground beef
- 1 celery stalk (chopped)
- 2 tbsp ketch up
- 2 tsp Worcestershire sauce
- 1 small onions (chopped)
- 1 green bell pepper (chopped)
- 1 tbsp sugar free maple syrup
- 1 cup tomato sauce (7.9 ounce)

- 2 garlic cloves (minced)
- ½ tsp salt or to taste
- ½ tsp ground black pepper or to taste

Directions:

For the chaffle:

1. Plug the waffle maker and preheat it. Spray it with non-stick spray.
2. Combine the baking powder, nutmeg, flour and onion powder in a mixing bowl. Add the eggs and mix.
3. Add the cheese and mix until the ingredients are well combined and you have formed a smooth batter.
4. Pour the batter into the waffle maker and spread it out to the edges of the waffle maker to cover all the holes on it.
5. Close the waffle lid and cook for about 5 minutes or according to waffle maker's settings.
6. After the cooking cycle, remove the chaffle from the waffle maker with a plastic or silicone utensil. Transfer the chaffle to a wire rack to cool.

For the sloppy joe filling:

1. Heat up a large skillet over medium to high heat.
2. Add the ground beef and saute until the beef is browned.
3. Use a slotted spoon to transfer the ground beef to a paper towel lined plate to drain. Drain all the grease in the skillet.
4. Add the olive oil to the skillet and heat it up.
5. Add the onions, green pepper, celery and garlic. Saute until the veggies are tender, stirring often to prevent burning.

6. Stir in the tomato sauce, Worcestershire sauce, ketchup, maple syrup, salt and pepper.

7. Add the browned beef and bring the mixture to a boil. Reduce the heat and simmer for about 10 minutes.

8. Remove the skillet from heat.

9. Scoop the sloppy joe into the chaffles and enjoy.

Nutrition Facts	
Servings: 2	
Amount per serving	
Calories	**698**
% Daily Value*	
Total Fat 30.5g	39%
Saturated Fat 8.4g	42%
Cholesterol 299mg	100%
Sodium 1692mg	74%
Total Carbohydrate 26.2g	10%
Dietary Fiber 5.5g	20%
Total Sugars 15.3g	
Protein 80.2g	
Vitamin D 9mcg	44%
Calcium 124mg	10%
Iron 46mg	254%
Potassium 1683mg	36%

KETO BLUEBERRY CHAFFLE

PREP TIME: 5 minutes

COOK TIME: 5 minutes

SERVINGS: 1

Ingredients:

- ¼ cups frozen blueberries
- 1 tbsp swerve
- ½ cup shredded mozzarella cheese
- 1 tbsp almond flour
- 1 egg (beaten)
- ½ tsp ground ginger
- ½ tsp vanilla extract

Topping:

- ½ cup heavy cream
- 1 tsp cinnamon

Directions:

1. Plug the waffle maker to preheat it and spray it with non-stick spray.
2. In a large mixing bowl, combine the swerve, almond flour and ginger. Add the egg, vanilla extract and cheese. Mix until the ingredients are well combined.
3. Gently fold in the blueberries.

4. Fill the waffle maker with the batter and spread it out to the edges of the waffle maker to cover all the holes on it.

5. Cover the lid of the waffle maker and bake for about 5 minutes or according to waffle maker's settings.

6. After the cooking cycle, remove the chaffle from the waffle maker using a plastic or silicone utensil.

7. Repeat step 4 to 6 until you have cooked all the batter into waffles.

8. Combine the heavy whipping cream and cinnamon in a mixing bowl.

9. Top the chaffle with the heavy cream mixture and serve.

10. Enjoy.

Nutrition Facts	
Servings: 1	
Amount per serving	
Calories	351
% Daily Value*	
Total Fat 29.3g	38%
Saturated Fat 16.7g	84%
Cholesterol 253mg	84%
Sodium 170mg	7%
Total Carbohydrate 12.5g	5%
Dietary Fiber 2.2g	8%
Total Sugars 4.4g	
Protein 11.2g	
Vitamin D 47mcg	233%
Calcium 97mg	7%

Nutrition Facts

Servings: 1

Iron 2mg	9%
Potassium 157mg	3%

BLT Chaffle Sandwich

PREP TIME: 5 minutes

COOK TIME: 10 minutes

SERVINGS: 1

Ingredients:

Sandwich Filling:

- 2 strips of bacon
- A pinch of salt
- 2 slices tomato
- 1 tbsp mayonnaise
- 3 pieces lettuce

Chaffle:

- 1 egg (beaten)
- ½ cup shredded mozzarella cheese
- ¼ tsp onion powder
- ¼ tsp garlic powder
- ½ tsp curry powder

Directions:

1. Plug the waffle maker and preheat it. Spray it with a non-stick spray.

2. In a mixing bowl, combine the cheese, onion powder, garlic and curry powder. Add the egg and mix until the ingredients are well combined.

3. Fill the waffle maker with the batter and spread the batter to the edges of the waffle maker to cover all the holes on the waffle iron.

4. Close the lid of the waffle maker and cook for about 4 minutes or according to waffle maker's settings.

5. After the cooking cycle, remove the chaffle from the waffle maker using a silicone or plastic utensil.

6. Repeat step 3 to 5 until you have cooked all the batter into chaffles. Set the chaffles aside to cool.

7. Heat up a skillet over medium heat. Add the bacon strips and sear until all sides of the bacon is browned, turning and pressing the bacon while searing.

8. Use a slotted spoon to transfer the bacon to a paper towel lined plate to drain.

9. Place the chaffles on a flat surface and spread mayonnaise over the face of the chaffles.

10. Divide the lettuce into two and layer it on one portion on both chaffles.

11. Layer the tomatoes on one of the chaffles and sprinkle with salt. Layer the bacon over the tomatoes and place the other chaffle over the one containing the bacon.

12. Press and serve immediately. Enjoy!!!

Nutrition Facts	
Servings: 1	
Amount per serving	
Calories	377

Nutrition Facts

Servings: 1

% Daily Value*

Total Fat 30g	39%
Saturated Fat 9.6g	48%
Cholesterol 175mg	58%
Sodium 1010mg	44%
Total Carbohydrate 7.8g	3%
Dietary Fiber 0.9g	3%
Total Sugars 2.7g	
Protein 18.4g	
Vitamin D 15mcg	77%
Calcium 46mg	4%
Iron 2mg	11%
Potassium 194mg	4%

KETO PIZZA CHAFFLE

PREP TIME: 10 minutes

COOK TIME: 15 minutes

SERVINGS: 2

Ingredients:

Pizza Filing:

- 1/3 cups pepperoni slices
- 1 tbsp marinara sauce
- ½ cup shredded mozzarella cheese
- 1 onion (finely chopped)
- 1 small green bell pepper (finely chopped)

Chaffle:

- 1 egg (beaten)
- A pinch of Italian seasoning
- A pinch of salt
- ½ cup mozzarella cheese
- ¼ tsp baking powder
- ½ tsp dried basil
- A pinch of garlic powder
- 1 tbsp + 1 tsp almond flour

Directions:

1. Preheat the oven to 400°F and line a baking sheet with parchment paper.

2. Plug the waffle maker and preheat it. Spray it with a nonstick spray.

3. **For the chaffle:** In a mixing bowl, combine the baking powder, almond flour, garlic powder, Italian seasoning, basil, mozzarella cheese and salt. Add the egg and mix until the ingredients are well combined.

4. Fill the waffle maker with appropriate amount of the batter and spread the batter to the edges of the waffle maker to cover all the holes on the waffle maker.

5. Close the lid of the waffle maker and cook for about 5 minutes or according to waffle maker's settings.

6. After the baking cycle, remove the chaffle from waffle maker with a silicone or plastic utensil.

7. Repeat step 4 to 6 until you have cooked all the batter into chaffles.

8. Top each of the chaffles with the marinara sauce, sprinkle the finely chopped onions and pepper over the chaffles.

9. Top with shredded mozzarella cheese and layer the pepperoni slices on the cheese topping.

10. Gently place the chaffles on the lined baking sheet. Place the baking sheet in the oven and bake for about 5 minutes. Afterwards, broil for about 1 minute.

11. Remove the pizza chaffles from the oven and let them cook for a few minutes.

12. Serve warm and enjoy.

Nutrition Facts
Servings: 2

Amount per serving

Calories	325

% Daily Value*

Total Fat 23.2g	30%
Saturated Fat 6.5g	32%
Cholesterol 116mg	39%
Sodium 648mg	28%
Total Carbohydrate 14.9g	5%
Dietary Fiber 3.7g	13%
Total Sugars 6.8g	
Protein 16.8g	
Vitamin D 10mcg	50%
Calcium 104mg	8%
Iron 2mg	10%
Potassium 383mg	8%

GARLIC BREAD CHAFFLE

PREP TIME: 5 minutes

COOK TIME: 15 minutes

SERVINGS: 2

Ingredients:

- 1 tbsp + 1 tsp almond flour
- 1 egg
- ¼ tsp baking powder
- ½ tsp garlic powder
- 1/8 tsp Italian seasoning
- 1 tbsp finely chopped cooked beef liver
- ¼ tsp garlic salt
- 3 tsp unsalted butter (melted)
- ½ cup shredded mozzarella cheese
- 2 tbsp shredded parmesan cheese

Garnish:

- Chopped green onion

Directions:

1. Preheat the oven to 375°F and line a baking sheet with parchment paper.
2. Plug the waffle maker to preheat it and spray it with non-stick spray.

3. In a mixing bowl, combine the almond flour, baking powder, Italian seasoning, garlic powder, beef liver and cheese. Add the egg and mix until the ingredients are well combined.

4. Fill the waffle maker with appropriate amount of the batter and spread the batter to the edges of the waffle maker to cover all the holes on the waffle iron.

5. Close the lid of the waffle maker and cook for about 3 to 4 minutes or according to waffle maker's settings.

6. Meanwhile, whisk together the garlic salt and melted butter in a bowl.

7. After the cooking cycle, remove the chaffle from the waffle iron with a plastic or silicone utensil.

8. Repeat step 4, 5 and 7 until you have cooked all the batter into chaffles.

9. Brush the butter mixture over the face of each chaffle.

10. Top the chaffles with parmesan cheese and arrange them into the line baking sheet.

11. Place the sheet in the oven and bake for about 5 minutes or until the cheese melts.

12. Remove the bread chaffles from the oven and leave them to cool for a few minutes.

13. Serve warm and top with chopped green onions.

Nutrition Facts	
Servings: 2	
Amount per serving	
Calories	218
% Daily Value*	
Total Fat 18g	23%

Nutrition Facts
Servings: 2

Saturated Fat 6.6g	33%
Cholesterol 112mg	37%
Sodium 840mg	37%
Total Carbohydrate 4.5g	2%
Dietary Fiber 1.6g	6%
Total Sugars 0.9g	
Protein 12g	
Vitamin D 12mcg	58%
Calcium 130mg	10%
Iron 2mg	13%
Potassium 131mg	3%

Keto Avocado Chaffle Toast

PREP TIME: 5 minutes

COOK TIME: 8 minutes

SERVINGS: 1

Ingredients:

Avocado Topping:

- 1 tbsp butter
- 1 green bell pepper (finely chopped)
- ½ cup feta cheese
- ½ avocado
- 1 tsp lemon juice
- ¼ tsp nutmeg
- ¼ tsp onion powder
- ½ tsp ground black pepper or to taste

Chaffle:

- ½ mozzarella cheese
- 1 egg (beaten)
- 1 tbsp Almond flour
- 1 tsp cinnamon
- ½ tsp baking soda

Directions:

1. Plug the waffle maker tom preheat it and spray it with a non-stick spray.

2. In a mixing bowl, combine the mozzarella, almond flour, baking soda and cinnamon. Add the egg and mix until the ingredients are well combined and you form a smooth batter.

3. Fill the waffle maker with appropriate amount of the batter and spread the batter to the edges of the waffle maker to cover all the holes on the waffle iron.

4. Close the lid of the waffle maker and cook for about 3 to 4 minutes or according to waffle maker's settings.

5. Meanwhile, dice the avocado into a bowl and mash until smooth. Add the bell pepper, nutmeg, onion powder, ground pepper and lemon juice. Mix until well combined.

6. After the baking cycle, remove the chaffle the waffle maker with a silicone or plastic utensil.

7. Repeat step 3, 4 and 6 until you have cooked all the batter into chaffles.

8. Brush the butter over the chaffles. Spread the avocado mixture over the chaffles. Top with shredded feta cheese.

9. Serve and enjoy.

Nutrition Facts	
Servings: 1	
Amount per serving	
Calories	820
% Daily Value*	
Total Fat 68.6g	88%

Nutrition Facts

Servings: 1

Saturated Fat 26.7g	133%
Cholesterol 268mg	89%
Sodium 1716mg	75%
Total Carbohydrate 31g	11%
Dietary Fiber 13g	46%
Total Sugars 11.5g	
Protein 29.8g	
Vitamin D 23mcg	117%
Calcium 520mg	40%
Iron 4mg	23%
Potassium 857mg	18%

Ham Chaffle

PREP TIME: 5 minutes

COOK TIME: 5 minutes

SERVINGS: 1

Ingredients:

- 1 large egg
- 4 tbsp chopped ham steak
- 1 scallion (chopped)
- ½ cup shredded mozzarella cheese
- ¼ tsp garlic salt
- 1/8 tsp Italian seasoning
- ½ jalapeno pepper (chopped)

Directions:

1. Plug the waffle maker to preheat it and spray it with a non-stick spray.
2. In a mixing bowl, combine the cheese, Italian seasoning, jalapeno, scallion, ham and garlic salt. Add the egg and mix until the ingredients are well combined.
3. Fill the waffle maker with an appropriate amount of the batter. Spread the batter to the edges of the waffle maker to cover all the holes on it.
4. Close the waffle maker and cook for about 4 minutes or according to waffle maker's settings.

5. After the cooking cycle, remove the chaffle from the waffle maker with plastic or silicone utensil.

6. Serve and enjoy.

Nutrition Facts Servings: 1	
Amount per serving	
Calories	**178**
% Daily Value*	
Total Fat 10.6g	14%
Saturated Fat 4.1g	20%
Cholesterol 213mg	71%
Sodium 598mg	26%
Total Carbohydrate 4.3g	2%
Dietary Fiber 1.1g	4%
Total Sugars 1.2g	
Protein 16.4g	
Vitamin D 18mcg	88%
Calcium 57mg	4%
Iron 2mg	9%
Potassium 228mg	5%

RASPBERRY CHAFFLE

PREP TIME: 10 minutes

COOK TIME: 8 minutes

SERVINGS: 1

Ingredients:

- 1 large egg (beaten)
- 1 tsp cinnamon
- 2 tbsp cream cheese
- ½ tsp vanilla extract
- 2 tbsp heavy cream
- 2 tbsp almond flour
- ¼ tsp baking powder
- 1/3 cup raspberries
- 2 tsp swerve sweetener or to taste
- 1/8 tsp salt

Directions:

1. Plug the waffle maker to preheat it and spray it with a non-stick spray.
2. In a medium mixing bowl, combine the cinnamon, almond flour, baking powder, 1 tsp swerve and salt.
3. In another mixing bowl, combine the cream cheese, egg and vanilla extract.

4. Pour the cream cheese mixture into the cheese mixture and mix until well combine and you have formed a smooth batter.

5. Fold in half of the raspberries.

6. Fill the waffle maker with an appropriate amount of the batter. Spread out the batter to cover all the holes on the waffle maker.

7. Close the waffle maker and cook for about 3-4 minutes or according to waffle maker's settings.

8. After the cooking cycle, use a plastic or silicone utensil to remove the chaffle from the waffle maker.

9. Repeat 6 to 7 until you have cooked all the batter into chaffles.

10. In a mixing bowl, combine the remaining swerve and heavy cream. Whisk until you form soft peak.

11. Spread the cream cheese mixture over the chaffles and top with the remaining raspberries.

12. Serve and enjoy.

Nutrition Facts	
Servings: 1	
Amount per serving	
Calories	**369**
% Daily Value*	
Total Fat 30.4g	39%
Saturated Fat 13.4g	67%
Cholesterol 249mg	83%
Sodium 433mg	19%
Total Carbohydrate 16.4g	6%

Nutrition Facts

Servings: 1

Dietary Fiber 5.4g	19%
Total Sugars 3.1g	
Protein 12g	
Vitamin D 33mcg	166%
Calcium 180mg	14%
Iron 2mg	13%
Potassium 315mg	7%

CAULIFLOWER TURKEY CHAFFLE

PREP TIME: 5 minutes

COOK TIME: 12 minutes

SERVINGS: 2

Ingredients:

- 1 large egg (beaten)
- ½ cup cauliflower rice
- ¼ cup diced turkey
- ½ tsp coconut aminos or soy sauce
- A pinch of ground black pepper
- A pinch of white pepper
- ¼ tsp curry
- ¼ tsp oregano
- 1 tbsp butter (melted)
- ¾ cup shredded mozzarella cheese
- 1 garlic clove (crushed)

Directions:

1. Plug the waffle maker to preheat it and spray it with a non-stick spray.
2. In a mixing bowl, combine the cauliflower rice, white pepper, black pepper, curry and oregano.
3. In another mixing bowl, whisk together the eggs, butter, crushed garlic and coconut aminos.

4. Pour the egg mixture into the cheese mixture and mix until the ingredients are well combined.

5. Add the diced turkey and stir to combine.

6. Sprinkle 2 tbsp cheese over the waffle maker. Fill the waffle maker with an appropriate amount of the batter. Spread out the batter to the edges to cover all the holes on the waffle maker. Sprinkle another 2 tbsp cheese over the batter.

7. Close the waffle maker and cook for about 4 minutes or according to waffle maker's settings.

8. After the cooking cycle, use a plastic or silicone utensil to remove the chaffle from the waffle maker.

9. Repeat step 6 to 8 until you have cooked all the batter into chaffles.

10. Serve warm and enjoy.

Nutrition Facts	
Servings: 2	
Amount per serving	
Calories	168
% Daily Value*	
Total Fat 11.5g	15%
Saturated Fat 6.1g	30%
Cholesterol 127mg	42%
Sodium 184mg	8%
Total Carbohydrate 3.8g	1%
Dietary Fiber 0.2g	1%
Total Sugars 1.2g	

Nutrition Facts

Servings: 2

Protein 12.5g

Vitamin D 13mcg	64%
Calcium 30mg	2%
Iron 2mg	13%
Potassium 101mg	2%

CHAFFLE TACOS

PREP TIME: 10 minutes

COOK TIME: 15 minutes

SERVINGS: 4

Ingredients:

Chaffle:

- 2 tbsp coconut flour
- 3 eggs (beaten)
- ½ cup shredded mozzarella cheese
- ½ cup shredded cheddar cheese
- A pinch of salt
- ½ tsp oregano

Taco Filling:

- 1 garlic clove (minced)
- 1 small onion (finely chopped)
- ½ pound ground beef
- 1 tsp olive oil
- 1 tsp cumin
- ½ tsp Italian seasoning
- 1 tsp paprika
- 1 tsp chili powder
- 1 roma tomato (diced)

- 1 green bell pepper (diced)
- 4 tbsp sour cream
- 1 tbsp chopped green onions

Directions:

1. . Plug the waffle maker to preheat it and spray it with a non-stick cooking spray.
2. In a mixing bowl, combine the mozzarella cheese, cheddar, coconut flour, salt and oregano. Add the eggs and mix until the ingredients are well combined.
3. Fill the waffle maker with an appropriate amount of the batter. Spread the batter to the edges to cover all the hole on the waffle maker.
4. Close the waffle maker and cook for about 5 minutes or according to waffle maker's settings.
5. After the cooking cycle, use a plastic or silicone utensil to remove the chaffle from the waffle maker. Set aside.
6. Repeat step 3 to 5 until you have cooked all the batter into chaffles.
7. Heat up a large skillet over medium to high heat.
8. Add the ground beef and saute until it is browned, breaking it apart while sautéing. Transfer the beef to a paper towel lined plate to drain and wipe the skillet clean.
9. Add the olive oil and leave it to get hot.
10. Add the onions and garlic and saute for 3-4 minutes or until the onion is translucent, stirring often.
11. Add the diced tomatoes and green pepper. Cook for 1 minute.
12. Add the browned ground beef. Stir in the cumin, paprika, chili powder and Italian seasoning.

13. Reduce the heat and cook on low for about 8 minutes, stirring often to prevent burning.
14. Remove the skillet from heat.
15. Scoop the taco mixture into the chaffles and top with chopped green onion and sour cream.
16. Enjoy.

Nutrition Facts	
Servings: 4	
Amount per serving	
Calories	**321**
% Daily Value*	
Total Fat 17.5g	22%
Saturated Fat 8.5g	43%
Cholesterol 196mg	65%
Sodium 266mg	12%
Total Carbohydrate 12.6g	5%
Dietary Fiber 4.4g	16%
Total Sugars 4.5g	
Protein 28.6g	
Vitamin D 13mcg	66%
Calcium 156mg	12%
Iron 13mg	74%
Potassium 533mg	11%

TUNA SALAD CHAFFLES

PREP TIME: 5 minutes

COOK TIME: 8 minutes

SERVINGS: 2

Ingredients:

Tuna Sandwich:

- 1 can water packed tuna (drained)
- 1 small sweet onion (chopped)
- 1 green bell pepper (finely chopped)
- 1 small carrot (peeled and chopped)
- 2 tbsp mayonnaise
- ½ tsp paprika
- ¼ tsp ground black pepper or to taste
- ¼ tsp salt or to taste
- 1 celery stalk (chopped)
- 1 tbsp freshly chopped parsley

Chaffle:

- 2 eggs (beaten)
- 4 tbsp almond flour
- 1 cup shredded mozzarella cheese
- ¾ tsp baking powder
- ½ tsp garlic powder

Directions:

1. Plug the waffle maker to preheat it and spray the it with a non-stick cooking spray.
2. In a mixing bowl, combine the almond flour, baking powder, garlic powder and mozzarella. Add the eggs and mix until the ingredients are well combined.
3. Fill the waffle maker with an appropriate amount of the batter and spread the batter to the edges to cover all the holes on the waffle maker.
4. Close the waffle maker and cook for about 4 minutes or according to waffle maker's settings.
5. After the cooking cycle, use a silicone or plastic utensil to remove the chaffle from the waffle maker.
6. Repeat step 3 to 5 until you have cooked all the batter into chaffles.
7. In a mixing bowl, combine the tuna, celery, pepper, onion, salt, paprika, carrot, onion and green pepper. Add the mayonnaise and toss until the ingredients are well combined.
8. Place one of the chaffle of a flat surface and spoon ½ of the tuna salad into it. Top with fresh parsley. Cover it with another chaffle and press.
9. Repeat step 8 to make the second sandwich.
10. Serve and enjoy.

Nutrition Facts
Servings: 2

Amount per serving
Calories   456

% Daily Value*

Nutrition Facts
Servings: 2

Total Fat 26.3g	34%
Saturated Fat 5.6g	28%
Cholesterol 203mg	68%
Sodium 610mg	27%
Total Carbohydrate 19.6g	7%
Dietary Fiber 4.1g	15%
Total Sugars 7.7g	
Protein 37.8g	
Vitamin D 15mcg	77%
Calcium 177mg	14%
Iron 3mg	16%
Potassium 824mg	18%

CUBAN PORK SANDWICH

PREP TIME: 10 minutes

COOK TIME: 10 minutes

SERVINGS: 1

Ingredients:

Sandwich Filling:

- 25 g swiss cheese (sliced)
- 2 ounces cooked deli ham (thinly sliced)
- 3 slices pickle chips
- ½ tbsp Dijon mustard
- ½ tbsp mayonnaise
- 3 ounces pork roast
- 1 tsp paprika
- 1 stalk celery (diced)

Chaffle:

- 1 tsp baking powder
- 1 large egg (beaten)
- 1 tbsp full-fat Greek yogurt
- 4 tbsp mozzarella cheese
- 1 tbsp almond flour

Directions:

1. Preheat the oven to 350°F and grease a baking sheet.

2. Plug the waffle maker to preheat it and spray it with a non-stick cooking spray.

3. In a mixing bowl, combine the almond flour, cheese and baking powder.

4. Add the egg and yogurt. Mix until the ingredients are well combined.

5. Fill the waffle maker with an appropriate amount of the batter and spread the batter to the edges to cover all the holes on the waffle maker.

6. Close the waffle maker and cook the waffle until it is crispy. That will take about 5 minutes. The time may vary in some waffle makers.

7. After the cooking cycle, remove the chaffle from the waffle maker with a plastic or silicone utensil.

8. Repeat step 4 to 6 until you have cooked all the batter into chaffles.

9. In a small mixing bowl, combine the mustard, oregano and mayonnaise.

10. Brush the mustard-mayonnaise mixture over the surface of both chaffles.

11. Layer the pork, ham, pickles and celery over one of the chaffles. Layer the cheese slices on top and cover it with the second chaffle.

12. Place it on the baking sheet. Place it in oven and bake until the cheese melts. You can place a heavy stainless place over the chaffle to make the sandwich come out flat after baking

13. After the baking cycle, remove the chaffle sandwich from the oven and let it cool for a few minutes.

14. Serve warm and enjoy.

Nutrition Facts	
Servings: 1	
Amount per serving	
Calories	**865**
% Daily Value*	
Total Fat 52.3g	67%
Saturated Fat 23.9g	119%
Cholesterol 379mg	126%
Sodium 2201mg	96%
Total Carbohydrate 17.3g	6%
Dietary Fiber 2.9g	10%
Total Sugars 2.7g	
Protein 82.6g	
Vitamin D 29mcg	143%
Calcium 599mg	46%
Iron 4mg	22%
Potassium 1201mg	26%

VEGETARIAN CHAFFLE SANDWICH

PREP TIME: 10 minutes

COOK TIME: 8 minutes

SERVINGS: 2

Ingredients:

Chaffle:

- 1 large egg (beaten)
- 1/8 tsp onion powder
- 1 tbsp almond flour
- ½ cup shredded mozzarella cheese
- 1 tsp nutmeg
- ¼ tsp baking powder

Sandwich Filling:

- ½ cup shredded carrot
- ½ cup sliced cucumber
- ½ medium bell pepper (sliced)
- 1 cup mixed salad greens
- ½ avocado (mashed and divided)
- 6 tbsp keto friendly hummus

Directions:

For the chaffle:

1. Plug the waffle maker to preheat it. Spray it with non-stick cooking spray.
2. Combine the baking powder, nutmeg, flour and onion powder in a mixing bowl. Add the eggs and mix.
3. Add the cheese and mix until the ingredients are well combined and you have formed a smooth batter.
4. Pour the batter into the waffle maker and spread it out to the edges of the waffle maker to cover all the holes on it.
5. Close the waffle lid and cook for about 5 minutes or according to waffle maker's settings.
6. After the cooking cycle, remove the chaffle from the waffle maker with a plastic or silicone utensil.
7. **For the sandwich:** Add 3 tablespoons of hummus to one chaffle and spread with a spoon.
8. Fill another chaffle with one half of the mashed avocado.
9. Fill the first chaffle slice with ¼ cup sliced cucumber, ½ cup mixed salad greens, ¼ cup shredded carrot and one half of the sliced bell pepper.
10. Place the chaffle on top and press lightly.
11. Repeat step 7 to 10 for the remaining ingredients to make the second sandwich.
12. Serve and enjoy.

Nutrition Facts	
Servings: 2	
Amount per serving	
Calories	293

Nutrition Facts
Servings: 2

% Daily Value*

Total Fat 22g	28%
Saturated Fat 4.4g	22%
Cholesterol 97mg	32%
Sodium 157mg	7%
Total Carbohydrate 17.8g	6%
Dietary Fiber 6.6g	24%
Total Sugars 4.6g	
Protein 11.3g	
Vitamin D 9mcg	44%
Calcium 110mg	8%
Iron 2mg	12%
Potassium 652mg	14%

CHAFFLE WITH SAUSAGE GRAVY

PREP TIME: 10 minutes

COOK TIME: 15 minutes

SERVINGS: 2

Ingredients:

Sausage Gravy:

- ¼ cup cooked breakfast sausage
- 1/8 tsp onion powder
- 1/8 tsp garlic powder
- ½ tsp pepper or more to taste
- 3 tbsp chicken broth
- 2 tsp cream cheese
- 2 tbsp heavy whipping cream
- ¼ tsp oregano

Chaffle:

- 1 tbsp almond flour
- 1 tbsp finely chopped onion
- 1/8 tsp salt
- ¼ tsp baking powder
- ½ cup mozzarella cheese
- 1 egg (beaten)

Directions:

1. Plug the waffle maker to preheat it and spray it with a non-stick spray.

2. In a mixing bowl, combine the almond flour, chopped onion, mozzarella, baking powder and salt. Add the egg and mix until the ingredients are well combined.

3. Fill the waffle maker with ½ of the batter and spread the batter to the edges to cover all the holes on the waffle maker.

4. Close the waffle maker and bake for about 4 minutes or according to waffle maker's settings.

5. After the baking cycle, remove the chaffle from the waffle maker with a silicone or plastic utensil.

6. Repeat step 3 to 5 until you have cooked all the batter into chaffles.

7. Heat up a skillet over medium to high heat. Add cooked sausage and sear until the sausage is browned, stirring often to prevent burning.

8. Pour in the chicken broth and add the oregano, garlic powder, onion powder, pepper, cream cheese and whipping cream.

9. Bring to a boil, reduce the heat and simmer for about 7 minutes or until the gravy sauce thickens.

10. Serve the chaffles with the gravy and enjoy.

Nutrition Facts	
Servings: 2	
Amount per serving	
Calories	198
% Daily Value*	

Nutrition Facts

Servings: 2

Total Fat 16.6g	21%
Saturated Fat 7.3g	36%
Cholesterol 123mg	41%
Sodium 429mg	19%
Total Carbohydrate 3.3g	1%
Dietary Fiber 0.8g	3%
Total Sugars 0.7g	
Protein 9.8g	
Vitamin D 16mcg	78%
Calcium 74mg	6%
Iron 1mg	6%
Potassium 195mg	4%

Sweet Brownie Chaffle

PREP TIME: 10 minutes

COOK TIME: 14 minutes

SERVINGS: 2

Ingredients:

- 1 large egg
- ¼ tsp baking powder
- ½ tsp vanilla extract
- ½ tsp ginger
- 2 tbsp cream cheese (melted)
- 1 ½ tsp cocoa powder
- 1 tbsp swerve

Topping:

- ½ tsp vanilla extract.
- ½ tsp cinnamon
- ¼ tsp liquid stevia
- 2 tbsp heavy cream
- 6 tbsp cream cheese (melted)

Directions:

1. Plug the waffle maker to preheat it and spray it with a non-stick cooking spray.

2. In a mixing bowl, combine the swerve, cocoa powder, ginger and baking powder.

3. In another mixing bowl, whisk together the cream cheese, egg and vanilla.

4. Pour the cocoa powder mixture into the egg mixture and mix until the ingredients are well combined.

5. Fill the waffle maker with an appropriate amount of batter and spread the batter to the edges to cover all the holes on the waffle maker.

6. Close the waffle maker and cook for about 7 minutes or according to your waffle maker's settings.

7. After the cooking cycle, use a silicone or plastic utensil to remove the chaffle from the waffle maker. Set aside to cool completely

8. Repeat step 5 to 7 until all the batter has been cooked into chaffles.

9. For the filling, combine the vanilla, cream cheese, stevia, cinnamon and heavy cream in a mixing bowl. Mix until well combined.

10. Spread the cream frosting over the surface of one chaffle and cover with another chaffle.

11. Place the filled chaffles in a refrigerator and chill for about 15 minutes.

12. Serve and enjoy.

Nutrition Facts	
Servings: 2	
Amount per serving	
Calories	240
% Daily Value*	

Nutrition Facts

Servings: 2

Total Fat 22.2g	28%
Saturated Fat 13.1g	66%
Cholesterol 158mg	53%
Sodium 160mg	7%
Total Carbohydrate 3.8g	1%
Dietary Fiber 0.8g	3%
Total Sugars 0.6g	
Protein 6.8g	
Vitamin D 17mcg	83%
Calcium 90mg	7%
Iron 1mg	7%
Potassium 202mg	4%

EGGNOG CHAFFLE

PREP TIME: 5 minutes

COOK TIME: 5 minutes

SERVINGS: 2

Ingredients:

- 2 tbsp coconut flour
- ½ tsp baking powder
- 1 tsp cinnamon
- 2 tbsp cream cheese
- 2 tsp swerve
- 1/8 tsp salt
- 1/8 tsp nutmeg
- 1 egg (beaten)
- 4 tbsp keto eggnog

Eggnog Filling:

- 4 tbsp keto eggnog
- ¼ tsp vanilla extract
- ¼ cup heavy cream
- 2 tsp granulated swerve
- 1/8 tsp nutmeg

Directions:

1. Plug the waffle maker to preheat it and spray it with a non-stick cooking spray.

2. Combine the coconut flour, baking powder, swerve, salt, cinnamon and nutmeg in a mixing bowl.

3. In another mixing bowl, whisk together the eggnog, cream cheese and egg.

4. Pour in the egg mixture into the flour mixture and mix until the ingredients are well combined.

5. Fill the waffle maker with an appropriate amount of the batter. Spread out the batter to cover all the holes on the waffle maker.

6. Close the waffle maker and cook for about 5 minutes or according to your waffle maker's settings.

7. After the baking cycle, remove the chaffle from the waffle maker with a plastic or silicone utensil.

8. Repeat step 5 to 7 until you have cooked all the batter into chaffles.

9. For the eggnog cream, whisk together the cream cheese, heavy cream, vanilla and eggnog. Add the swerve and nutmeg; mix until the ingredients are well combined.

10. Top the chaffles with the eggnog cream and enjoy

Nutrition Facts	
Servings: 2	
Amount per serving	
Calories	193
% Daily Value*	

Nutrition Facts	
Servings: 2	
Total Fat 12.1g	16%
Saturated Fat 6.9g	35%
Cholesterol 115mg	38%
Sodium 267mg	12%
Total Carbohydrate 16.1g	6%
Dietary Fiber 3.7g	13%
Total Sugars 3.4g	
Protein 6.9g	
Vitamin D 16mcg	78%
Calcium 171mg	13%
Iron 1mg	4%
Potassium 186mg	4%

CHICKEN JALAPENO POPPER CHAFFLE

PREP TIME: 5 minutes

COOK TIME: 10 minutes

SERVINGS: 2

Ingredients:

- 1 egg
- 1 small jalapeno pepper (sliced)
- 1 can chicken breast (diced)
- A pinch of salt
- A pinch of ground black pepper
- 1/8 tsp garlic powder
- 1/8 tsp onion powder
- 2 tbsp shredded parmesan cheese
- 4 tbsp shredded cheddar cheese
- 1 tsp cream cheese

Topping:

- Sour cream

Directions:

1. Plug the waffle maker to preheat it and spray it with a non-stick spray.

2. In a mixing bowl, combine parmesan, cheddar, jalapeno, salt, ground pepper, garlic powder and onion powder.

3. Whisk together the egg and cream cheese. Pour it into the cheese mixture and mix until the ingredients are well combined. Fold in the diced chicken.

4. Fill the waffle maker with about ½ of the batter and spread out the batter to cover all the holes on the waffle maker.

5. Close the waffle maker and cook for about 5 minutes or according to waffle maker's settings.

6. After the cooking cycle, use a plastic or silicone utensil to remove the chaffle from the waffle maker.

7. Repeat step 4 to 6 until the you have cooked all the batter into chaffles.

8. Serve warm and top with sour cream as desired.

Nutrition Facts	
Servings: 2	
Amount per serving	
Calories	**322**
% Daily Value*	
Total Fat 13.4g	17%
Saturated Fat 5g	25%
Cholesterol 217mg	72%
Sodium 357mg	16%
Total Carbohydrate 1.3g	0%
Dietary Fiber 0.2g	1%
Total Sugars 0.6g	

Nutrition Facts

Servings: 2

Protein 46.3g

Vitamin D 10mcg	48%
Calcium 188mg	14%
Iron 1mg	7%
Potassium 719mg	15%

BACON JALAPENO POPPER CHAFFLE

PREP TIME: 5 minutes

COOK TIME: 10 minutes

SERVINGS: 3

Ingredients:

- 4 slices bacon (diced)
- 3 eggs
- 3 tbsp coconut flour
- 1 tsp baking powder
- ¼ tsp salt
- ½ tsp oregano
- A pinch of onion powder
- A pinch of garlic powder
- ½ cup cream cheese
- 1 cup shredded cheddar cheese
- 2 jalapeno pepper (deseeded and chopped)
- ½ cup sour cream

Directions:

1. Plug the waffle maker to preheat it and spray it with a non-stick cooking spray.
2. Heat up a frying pan over medium to high heat. Add the bacon and saute until the bacon is brown and crispy.

3. Use a slotted spoon to transfer the bacon to a paper towel lined plate to drain.

4. In a mixing bowl, combine the coconut flour, baking powder, salt, oregano, onion and garlic.

5. In another mixing bowl, whisk together the egg and cream cheese until well combined.

6. Add the cheddar cheese and mix. Pour in the flour mixture and mix until you form a smooth batter.

7. Pour an appropriate amount of the batter into the waffle maker and spread the batter to the edges to cover all the holes on the waffle maker.

8. Close the waffle maker and cook for about 5 minutes or according to waffle maker's settings.

9. After the cooking cycle, use a plastic or silicone utensil to remove the chaffle from the waffle maker.

10. Repeat step 7 to 9 until you have cooked all the batter into chaffles.

11. Serve warm and top with sour cream, crispy bacon and jalapeno slices.

Nutrition Facts	
Servings: 3	
Amount per serving	
Calories	**635**
% Daily Value*	
Total Fat 51g	65%
Saturated Fat 28.3g	142%
Cholesterol 291mg	97%
Sodium 1241mg	54%

Nutrition Facts	
Servings: 3	
Total Carbohydrate 13.5g	5%
Dietary Fiber 5.4g	19%
Total Sugars 2.1g	
Protein 30.6g	
Vitamin D 20mcg	100%
Calcium 451mg	35%
Iron 2mg	13%
Potassium 535mg	11%

CHOCOLATE CANNOLI CHAFFLE

PREP TIME: 10 minutes

COOK TIME: 10 minutes

SERVINGS: 4

Ingredients:

Cannoli Topping:

- 2 tbsp granulated swerve
- 4 tbsp cream cheese
- ¼ tsp vanilla extract
- ¼ tsp cinnamon
- 6 tbsp ricotta cheese
- 1 tsp lemon juice

Chaffle:

- 3 tbsp almond flour
- 1 tbsp swerve
- 1 egg
- 1/8 tsp baking powder
- 3/4 tbsp butter (melted)
- ½ tsp nutmeg
- 1 tbsp sugar free chocolate chips
- 1/8 tsp vanilla extract

Directions:

1. Plug the waffle maker to preheat it and spray it with a non-stick spray.
2. In a mixing bowl, whisk together the egg, butter and vanilla extract.
3. In another mixing bowl, combine the almond flour, baking powder, nutmeg, chocolate chips and swerve.
4. Pour the egg mixture into the flour mixture and mix until the ingredients are well combined and you have formed a smooth batter.
5. Fill your waffle maker with an appropriate amount of the batter and spread out the batter to the edged to cover all the holes on the waffle maker.
6. Close the waffle maker and cook for about 4 minutes or according to waffle maker's settings.
7. After the baking cycle, remove the chaffle from the waffle maker with a plastic or silicone utensil.
8. Repeat step 5 to 7 until you have cooked all the batter into waffles.
9. For the topping, pour the cream cheese into a blender and add the ricotta, lemon juice, cinnamon, vanilla and swerve sweetener. Blend until smooth and fluffy.
10. Spread the cream over the chaffles and enjoy.

Nutrition Facts	
Servings: 4	
Amount per serving	
Calories	149
% Daily Value*	

Nutrition Facts

Servings: 4

Total Fat 11.7g	15%
Saturated Fat 5.5g	27%
Cholesterol 65mg	22%
Sodium 99mg	4%
Total Carbohydrate 5.7g	2%
Dietary Fiber 0.7g	3%
Total Sugars 0.3g	
Protein 6.1g	
Vitamin D 5mcg	27%
Calcium 87mg	7%
Iron 0mg	3%
Potassium 76mg	2%

CORNBREAD CHAFFLE

PREP TIME: 5 minutes

COOK TIME: 12 minutes

SERVINGS: 3

Ingredients:

- 1 ½ tbsp melted butter
- 3 tbsp almond flour
- 1 milliliter cornbread flavoring
- 2 tbsp Mexican blend cheese
- 2 tbsp shredded parmesan cheese
- 1 small jalapeno (seeded and sliced)
- 2 tsp swerve sweetener
- 1 large egg (beaten)
- ½ tsp all spice

Directions:

1. Plug the waffle maker to preheat it and spray it with a non-stick cooking spray.
2. In a mixing bowl, combine almond flour, jalapeno, all spice, baking powder and swerve.
3. In another mixing bowl, whisk together the egg, butter and cornbread flavoring.
4. Pour the egg mixture into the flour mixture and mix until you form a smooth batter. Stir in the cheese.

5. Sprinkle some parmesan cheese over the waffle maker. Pour an appropriate amount of the batter into the waffle maker and spread out the batter to the edges to cover all the holes on the waffle maker. Sprinkle some parmesan over the batter

6. Close the waffle maker and bake for about 5 minutes or according to you waffle maker's settings.

7. After the baking cycle, remove the chaffle from the waffle maker with a plastic or silicone utensil.

8. Repeat step 5 to 7 until you have cooked all the batter into chaffles.

9. Serve warm with your desired topping and enjoy.

Nutrition Facts	
Servings: 3	
Amount per serving	
Calories	**157**
% Daily Value*	
Total Fat 13.6g	17%
Saturated Fat 6.2g	31%
Cholesterol 86mg	29%
Sodium 172mg	7%
Total Carbohydrate 4.1g	1%
Dietary Fiber 1g	3%
Total Sugars 0.8g	
Protein 6.4g	
Vitamin D 10mcg	49%
Calcium 107mg	8%

Nutrition Facts	
Servings: 3	
Iron 1mg	4%
Potassium 42mg	1%

KETO GINGERBREAD CHAFFLE

PREP TIME: 5 minutes

COOK TIME: 8 minutes

SERVINGS: 2

Ingredients:

- 1 egg (beaten)
- 1/8 tsp garlic powder
- ¼ tsp nutmeg
- ½ tsp cinnamon
- ½ cup shredded mozzarella cheese
- 2 tsp granulated swerve
- ½ tsp baking powder
- 2 tbsp almond flour
- ½ tsp ginger

Topping:

- ½ cup heavy cream
- 1 tsp cinnamon
- 1 tsp sugar free maple syrup

Directions:

1. Plug the waffle maker to preheat it and spray it with a non-stick cooking spray.

2. In a medium mixing bowl, combine the almond flour, baking powder, cinnamon, garlic, ginger, nutmeg, swerve and cheese. Add the egg and mix until the ingredients are combined.

3. Pour an appropriate amount of the batter into the waffle maker and spread out the batter to the edged to cover all the holes on the waffle maker.

4. Close the waffle maker and cook for about 4 minutes or according to your waffle maker's settings.

5. After the cooking cycle, use a plastic or silicone utensil to remove the chaffle from the waffle maker.

6. Repeat step 2 to 5 until you have cooked all the batter into waffles. Let the chaffles sit for a few minutes to cool.

7. For the filling, combine the heavy cream, cinnamon and syrup in a mixing bowl. Mix until smooth and fluffy.

8. Top the chaffles with the cream mixture and serve.

Nutrition Facts	
Servings: 2	
Amount per serving	
Calories	208
% Daily Value*	
Total Fat 18.2g	23%
Saturated Fat 8.7g	43%
Cholesterol 127mg	42%
Sodium 87mg	4%
Total Carbohydrate 6.8g	2%
Dietary Fiber 1.2g	4%
Total Sugars 0.6g	

Nutrition Facts

Servings: 2

Protein 7g

Vitamin D 23mcg	117%
Calcium 112mg	9%
Iron 1mg	5%
Potassium 190mg	4%

ALMOND BUTTER CHAFFLE

PREP TIME: 10 minutes

COOK TIME: 20 minutes

SERVINGS: 4

Ingredients:

- 2 eggs (beaten)
- 3 tsp granulated swerve sweetener
- 4 tbsp almond flour
- ½ tsp vanilla extract
- ½ cup grated mozzarella cheese
- ½ cup parmesan cheese
- 1/8 tsp allspice

Almond Butter Filling:

- ½ tsp vanilla extract
- 4 tbsp almond butter
- 2 tbsp butter (melted)
- 2 tbsp swerve sweetener
- 1/8 tsp nutmeg

Directions:

1. Plug the waffle maker to preheat it and spray it with a non-stick cooking spray.

2. In a mixing bowl, combine the mozzarella, allspice, almond flour, and swerve sweetener. Add the egg and vanilla extract and mix until the ingredients are well combined.

3. Sprinkle some parmesan cheese over the waffle maker.

4. Pour an appropriate amount of the batter into the waffle and spread out the batter to cover all the holes on the waffle maker.

5. Sprinkle some parmesan over the batter.

6. Close the waffle maker and cook for about 5 minutes or according to your waffle maker's settings.

7. After the cooking cycle, use a plastic or silicone utensil to remove the chaffle from the waffle maker. Transfer the chaffle to a wire rack to cool.

8. Repeat step 3 to 7 until you have cooked all the batter into chaffles.

9. For the filling, combine butter, almond butter, swerve, vanilla and nutmeg. Mix until the mixture is smooth and fluffy.

10. Spread the cream over the surface of one chaffle and cover the with another chaffle. Repeat until you have filled all the chaffles.

11. Serve and enjoy.

Nutrition Facts Servings: 2	
Amount per serving	
Calories	**648**
% Daily Value*	
Total Fat 54.8g	70%

Nutrition Facts

Servings: 2

Saturated Fat 15.3g	76%
Cholesterol 216mg	72%
Sodium 438mg	19%
Total Carbohydrate 18.4g	7%
Dietary Fiber 6.8g	24%
Total Sugars 3.2g	
Protein 29.7g	
Vitamin D 23mcg	117%
Calcium 401mg	31%
Iron 3mg	18%
Potassium 67mg	1%

Pumpkin Pecan Chaffle

PREP TIME: 5 minutes

COOK TIME: 10 minutes

SERVINGS: 2

Ingredients:

- 2 tbsp toasted pecans (chopped)
- 2 tbsp almond flour
- 1 tbsp pumpkin puree
- ½ tsp pumpkin spice
- ½ cup grated mozzarella cheese
- 1 tsp granulated swerve sweetener
- 1 egg
- ½ tsp nutmeg
- ½ tsp vanilla extract
- ½ tsp baking powder

Directions:

1. Plug the waffle maker to preheat it and spray it with a non-stick spray.
2. In a mixing bowl, combine the almond flour, baking powder, pumpkin spice, swerve, cheese and nutmeg.
3. In another mixing bowl, whisk together the pumpkin puree egg and vanilla extract.

4. Pour the egg mixture into the flour mixture and mix until the ingredients are well combined.

5. Pour an appropriate amount of the batter into the waffle maker and spread out the batter to the edges to cover all the holes on the waffle maker.

6. Close the waffle maker and cook for about 5 minutes or according to your waffle maker's settings.

7. After the cooking cycle, use a silicone or plastic utensil to remove the chaffle from the waffle maker.

8. Repeat step 5 to 7 until you have cooked all the batter into chaffles.

9. Serve warm and top with whipped cream. Enjoy!!!

Nutrition Facts
Servings: 2

Amount per serving

Calories	175
% Daily Value*	
Total Fat 14.4g	18%
Saturated Fat 2.6g	13%
Cholesterol 86mg	29%
Sodium 75mg	3%
Total Carbohydrate 6.3g	2%
Dietary Fiber 2.2g	8%
Total Sugars 1.4g	
Protein 7.5g	
Vitamin D 8mcg	39%
Calcium 99mg	8%

Nutrition Facts	
Servings: 2	
Iron 1mg	7%
Potassium 219mg	5%

CEREAL AND WALNUT CHAFFLE

PREP TIME: 5 minutes

COOK TIME: 6 minutes

SERVINGS: 2

Ingredients:

- 1 milliliter of cereal flavoring
- ¼ tsp baking powder
- 1 tsp granulated swerve
- 1/8 tsp xanthan gum
- 1 tbsp butter (melted)
- ½ tsp coconut flour
- 2 tbsp toasted walnut (chopped)
- 1 tbsp cream cheese
- 2 tbsp almond flour
- 1 large egg (beaten)
- ¼ tsp cinnamon

- 1/8 tsp nutmeg

Directions:

1. Plug the waffle maker to preheat it and spray it with a non-stick spray.
2. In a mixing bowl, whisk together the egg, cereal flavoring, cream cheese and butter.
3. In another mixing bowl, combine the coconut flour, almond flour, cinnamon, nutmeg, swerve, xanthan gum and baking powder.
4. Pour the egg mixture into the flour mixture and mix until you form a smooth batter.
5. Fold in the chopped walnuts.
6. Pour in an appropriate amount of the batter into the waffle maker and spread out the batter to the edges to cover all the holes on the waffle maker.
7. Close the waffle maker and cook for about 3 minutes or according to your waffle maker's settings.
8. After the cooking cycle, use a plastic or silicone utensil to remove the chaffle from the waffle maker.
9. Repeat step 6 to 8 until you have cooked all the batter into chaffles.
10. Serve and top with sour cream or heavy cream.

Nutrition Facts	
Servings: 2	
Amount per serving	
Calories	**200**
% Daily Value*	
Total Fat 18.2g	23%

Nutrition Facts

Servings: 2

Saturated Fat 6.1g	31%
Cholesterol 114mg	38%
Sodium 92mg	4%
Total Carbohydrate 4.7g	2%
Dietary Fiber 1.8g	6%
Total Sugars 0.6g	
Protein 7.1g	
Vitamin D 13mcg	64%
Calcium 69mg	5%
Iron 1mg	6%
Potassium 148mg	3%

CINNAMON ROLL CHAFFLE

PREP TIME: 7 minutes

COOK TIME: 9 minutes

SERVINGS: 3 chaffles

Ingredients:

- 1 egg (beaten)
- ½ cup shredded mozzarella cheese
- 1 tsp cinnamon
- 1 tsp sugar free maple syrup
- ¼ tsp baking powder
- 1 tbsp almond flour
- ½ tsp vanilla extract

Topping:

- 2 tsp granulated swerve
- 1 tbsp heavy cream
- 4 tbsp cream cheese

Directions:

1. Plug the waffle maker to preheat it and spray it with a non-stick spray.
2. In a mixing bowl, whisk together the egg, maple syrup and vanilla extract.

3. In another mixing bowl, combine the cinnamon, almond flour, baking powder and mozzarella cheese.

4. Pour in the egg mixture into the flour mixture and mix until the ingredients are well combined.

5. Pour in an appropriate amount of the batter into the waffle maker and spread out the batter to the edges to cover all the holes on the waffle maker.

6. Close the waffle maker and bake for about 3 minute or according to your waffle maker's settings.

7. After the cooking cycle, use a silicone or plastic utensil to remove the chaffle from the waffle maker.

8. Repeat step 5 to 7 until you have cooked all the batter into chaffles.

9. For the topping, combine the cream cheese, swerve and heavy cream in a microwave safe dish.

10. Place the dish in a microwave and microwave on high until the mixture is melted and smooth. Stir every 15 seconds.

11. Top the chaffles with the cream mixture and enjoy.

Nutrition Facts	
Servings: 3	
Amount per serving	
Calories	**121**
% Daily Value*	
Total Fat 9.9g	13%
Saturated Fat 5.1g	26%
Cholesterol 79mg	26%
Sodium 92mg	4%

Nutrition Facts

Servings: 3

Total Carbohydrate 3.8g	1%
Dietary Fiber 0.7g	2%
Total Sugars 0.3g	
Protein 4.8g	
Vitamin D 8mcg	39%
Calcium 51mg	4%
Iron 1mg	3%
Potassium 86mg	2%

Chicken Parmesan Chaffle

PREP TIME: 5 minutes

COOK TIME: 13 minutes

SERVINGS: 2 chaffles

Ingredients:

- 1 egg (beaten)
- ½ cup shredded chicken
- 2 tbsp shredded parmesan cheese
- 1/3 cup shredded mozzarella cheese
- ¼ tsp garlic powder
- ¼ tsp onion powder
- 2 tbsp marinara sauce
- 1 tsp Italian seasoning

Garnish:

- 1 tbsp chopped green onions

Directions:

1. Plug the waffle maker to preheat it and spray it with a non-stick cooking spray.
2. In a mixing bowl, combine the mozzarella cheese, shredded chicken, Italian seasoning, onion powder and garlic powder. Add the egg and mix until the ingredients are well combined.

3. Pour half of the batter into the waffle maker and spread out the batter to the edges to cover all the holes on the waffle maker.

4. Close the waffle maker and cook for about 4 minutes or according to your waffle maker's settings.

5. Meanwhile, preheat your oven to 400°F and line a baking sheet with parchment paper.

6. After the cooking cycle, use a plastic or silicone utensil to remove the chaffle from the waffle maker.

7. Repeat 3, 4 and 6 to make the second chaffle.

8. Spread marinara sauce over the surface of both chaffles and sprinkle the parmesan cheese over the chaffles.

9. Arrange the chaffles into the baking sheet and place them in the oven. Bake for about 5 minutes or until the cheese melts.

10. Remove the chaffles from the oven and let them cool for a few minutes.

11. Serve and top with chopped green onion.

Nutrition Facts	
Servings: 2	
Amount per serving	
Calories	**144**
% Daily Value*	
Total Fat 6.7g	9%
Saturated Fat 2.7g	14%
Cholesterol 118mg	39%
Sodium 212mg	9%
Total Carbohydrate 3.7g	1%

Nutrition Facts

Servings: 2

Dietary Fiber 0.5g	2%
Total Sugars 2g	
Protein 16.9g	
Vitamin D 8mcg	39%
Calcium 89mg	7%
Iron 1mg	5%
Potassium 160mg	3%

CARROT CAKE CHAFFLE

PREP TIME: 10 minutes

COOK TIME: 18 minutes

SERVINGS: 10 (6 mini chaffles)

Ingredients:

- 1 tbsp toasted pecans (chopped)
- 2 tbsp granulated swerve
- 1 tsp pumpkin spice
- 1 tsp baking powder
- ½ shredded carrots
- 2 tbsp butter (melted)
- 1 tsp cinnamon
- 1 tsp vanilla extract (optional)
- 2 tbsp heavy whipping cream
- ¾ cup almond flour
- 1 egg (beaten)

Butter cream cheese frosting:

- ½ cup cream cheese (softened)
- ¼ cup butter (softened)
- ½ tsp vanilla extract
- ¼ cup granulated swerve

Directions:

1. Plug the chaffle maker to preheat it and spray it with a non-stick cooking spray.

2. In a mixing bowl, combine the almond flour, cinnamon, carrot, pumpkin spice and swerve.

3. In another mixing bowl, whisk together the eggs, butter, heavy whipping cream and vanilla extract.

4. Pour the flour mixture into the egg mixture and mix until you form a smooth batter.

5. Fold in the chopped pecans.

6. Pour in an appropriate amount of the batter into your waffle maker and spread out the batter to the edges to cover all the holes on the waffle maker.

7. Close the waffle maker and cook for about 3 minutes or according to your waffle maker's settings.

8. After the cooking cycle, use a plastic or silicone utensil to remove the chaffle from the waffle maker.

9. Repeat step 6 to 8 until you have cooked all the batter into chaffles.

10. For the frosting, combine the cream cheese and cutter int a mixer and mix until well combined.

11. Add the swerve and vanilla extract and slowly until the sweetener is well incorporated. Mix on high until the frosting is fluffy.

12. Place one chaffle on a flat surface and spread some cream frosting over it. Layer another chaffle over the first one a spread some cream over it too.

13. Repeat step 12 until you have assembled all the chaffles into a cake.

14. Cut and serve.

Nutrition Facts
Servings: 10

Amount per serving

Calories	181

% Daily Value*

Total Fat 17.4g	22%
Saturated Fat 8.1g	41%
Cholesterol 52mg	17%
Sodium 93mg	4%
Total Carbohydrate 4.5g	2%
Dietary Fiber 1.2g	4%
Total Sugars 0.6g	
Protein 3.5g	
Vitamin D 8mcg	39%
Calcium 61mg	5%
Iron 1mg	4%
Potassium 91mg	2%

SAVORY CHAFFLE STICK

PREP TIME: 10 minutes

COOK TIME: 25 minutes

SERVINGS: 16 chaffle sticks

Ingredients:

- 6 eggs
- 2 cups shredded mozzarella cheese
- A pinch of salt
- ½ tsp ground black pepper or to taste
- ½ tsp baking powder
- 4 tbsp coconut flour
- 1 tsp onion powder
- 1 tsp garlic powder
- 1 tsp oregano
- ¼ tsp Italian seasoning
- 1 tbsp olive oil
- 1 tbsp melted butter

Directions:

1. Plug the waffle maker to preheat it and spray it with a non-stick cooking spray.
2. Break 4 of the eggs into a mixing bowl and beat. Add the coconut flour, baking powder, salt, cheese and Italian

seasoning. Combine until the ingredients are well combined. Add more flour if the mixture is too thick.

3. Pour an appropriate amount of the batter into the waffle maker and spread out the batter to cover all the holes on the waffle maker.

4. Cover the waffle maker and cook for about 7 minutes or according to your waffle maker's settings. Make sure the chaffle is browned.

5. After the cooking cycle, use a plastic or silicone utensil to remove the chaffle form the waffle maker.

6. Repeat step 3 to 5 until you have cooked all the batter into chaffles.

7. Cut the chaffles into sticks. Each mini chaffle should make about 4 sticks.

8. Preheat the oven to 350°F. Line a baking sheet with parchment paper and grease it with the melted butter.

9. Break the remaining two eggs into another mixing bowl and beat.

10. In another mixing bowl, combine the oregano, pepper, garlic and onion.

11. Dip one chaffle stick into the egg. Bring it out and hold it for a few seconds to allow excess liquid to drip off.

12. Dip the wet chaffle stick into the seasoning mixture and make sure it is coated with seasoning. Drop it on the baking sheet.

13. Repeat step 11 and 12 until all the chaffle sticks are coated.

14. Arrange the chaffle sticks into the baking sheet in a single layer.

15. Place the baking sheet in the oven and bake for 10 minutes.

16. Remove the baking sheet from the oven, brush the oil over the sticks and flip them.
17. Return it to the oven and bake for an additional 6 minutes or until the stick are golden brown.
18. Remove the sticks from the oven and let them cool for a few minutes.
19. Serve and enjoy.

Nutrition Facts

Serving size: 1 chaffle stick

Servings: 16

Amount per serving	
Calories	**57**
% Daily Value*	
Total Fat 4.1g	5%
Saturated Fat 1.6g	8%
Cholesterol 65mg	22%
Sodium 61mg	3%
Total Carbohydrate 2g	1%
Dietary Fiber 0.8g	3%
Total Sugars 0.2g	
Protein 3.4g	
Vitamin D 6mcg	31%
Calcium 21mg	2%
Iron 0mg	2%
Potassium 44mg	1%

SHIRATAKI RICE CHAFFLE

PREP TIME: 5 minutes

COOK TIME: 20 minutes

SERVINGS: 4

Ingredients:

- 2 tbsp almond flour
- ½ tsp oregano
- 1 bag of shirataki rice
- 1 tsp baking powder
- 1 cup shredded cheddar cheese
- 2 eggs (beaten)

Directions:

1. Rinse the shirataki rice with warm water for about 30 seconds and rinse it.
2. Plug the waffle maker to preheat it and spray it with a non-stick cooking spray.
3. In a mixing bowl, combine the rinsed rice, almond flour, baking powder, oregano and shredded cheese. Add the eggs and mix until the ingredients are well combined.
4. Fill the waffle maker with an appropriate amount of the batter and spread out the batter to the edges to cover all the holes on the waffle maker.

5. Close the waffle make and cook for about 5 minutes or according to you waffle maker's settings.

6. After the cooking cycle, use a silicone or plastic utensil to remove the chaffles from the waffle maker.

7. Repeat step 4 to 6 until you have cooked all the batter into chaffles.

8. Serve and enjoy.

Nutrition Facts

Servings: 4

Amount per serving	
Calories	**168**
% Daily Value*	
Total Fat 13.2g	17%
Saturated Fat 6.8g	34%
Cholesterol 112mg	37%
Sodium 209mg	9%
Total Carbohydrate 2g	1%
Dietary Fiber 0.5g	2%
Total Sugars 0.3g	
Protein 10.6g	
Vitamin D 11mcg	55%
Calcium 272mg	21%
Iron 2mg	10%
Potassium 187mg	4%

Cauliflower Hash Brown Chaffle

PREP TIME: 10 minutes

COOK TIME: 8 minutes

SERVINGS: 2

Ingredients:

- 1 egg
- ½ cup cauliflower rice
- ¼ tsp onion powder
- ¼ tsp salt
- ½ tsp garlic powder
- 4 tbsp shredded cheddar cheese
- 1 green onion (chopped)

Directions:

1. Put the cauliflower rice in a microwave safe dish and cover the dish. Place the dish in the microwave and microwave for 3 minutes.
2. Remove the dish from the microwave and stir. Return it to the microwave and steam for about 1 minute or until tender.
3. Let the steamed cauliflower cool for a few minutes. Wrap the steamed cauliflower in a clean towel and squeeze it to remove excess water.

4. Plug the waffle maker to preheat it and spray it with a non-stick cooking spray.

5. In a mixing bowl, combine the cauliflower, green onion, onion powder, cheese, salt, garlic and salt. Add the egg and mix until the ingredients are well combined.

6. Fill your waffle maker with an appropriate amount of the batter and spread out the batter to cover all the holes on the waffle maker.

7. Close the waffle maker and cook until the chaffle is browned. This will take about 4 minutes or more depending on your waffle maker.

8. After the cooking cycle, use a plastic or silicone utensil to remove the chaffle from the waffle maker.

9. Repeat step 6 to 8 until you have cooked all the batter into waffles.

10. Serve the hash brown chaffles and top with your desired topping.

Nutrition Facts
Servings: 2

Amount per serving	
Calories	**102**
% Daily Value*	
Total Fat 6.9g	9%
Saturated Fat 3.7g	18%
Cholesterol 97mg	32%
Sodium 435mg	19%
Total Carbohydrate 2.9g	1%
Dietary Fiber 0.8g	3%

Nutrition Facts

Servings: 2

Total Sugars 1.2g

Protein 7.1g

Vitamin D 9mcg	47%
Calcium 126mg	10%
Iron 1mg	4%
Potassium 75mg	2%

STRAWBERRY SHORTCAKE CHAFFLE

PREP TIME: 5 minutes

COOK TIME: 8 minutes

SERVINGS: 2 chaffles

Ingredients:

- ½ tsp cinnamon
- ½ cup shredded mozzarella cheese
- 1 tsp sugar free maple syrup
- 2 tsp granulated swerve
- 1 egg (beaten)
- 1 tbsp almond flour

Topping:

- 3 fresh strawberries (sliced)
- 2 tsp granulated swerve
- 1 tbsp heavy cream
- ¼ tsp vanilla extract
- 4 tbsp cream cheese (softened)

Directions:

1. Plug the waffle maker to preheat it and spray it with a non-stick cooking spray.

2. In a mixing bowl, combine the cinnamon, swerve, cheese and almond flour. Add the egg and maple syrup. Mix until the ingredients are well combined.

3. Pour an appropriate amount of the batter into the waffle iron and spread the batter to the edges to cover all the holes on the waffle maker.

4. Close the waffle maker and cook for about 4 minutes or according to your waffle maker's settings.

5. After the cooking cycle, remove the chaffle from the waffle maker with a plastic or silicone utensil.

6. Repeat step 3 to 5 until you have cooked all the batter into chaffles.

7. For the topping, combine the cream cheese, swerve vanilla and heavy cream in a mixing bowl. Whisk until the mixture is smooth and fluffy.

8. Top the chaffles with the cream and sliced strawberries.

9. Serve and enjoy.

Nutrition Facts	
Servings: 2	
Amount per serving	
Calories	**180**
% Daily Value*	
Total Fat 15g	19%
Saturated Fat 7.7g	38%
Cholesterol 118mg	39%
Sodium 137mg	6%
Total Carbohydrate 5.2g	2%
Dietary Fiber 1.1g	4%

Nutrition Facts

Servings: 2

Total Sugars 1.3g

Protein 7.3g

Vitamin D 12mcg	58%
Calcium 54mg	4%
Iron 1mg	5%
Potassium 90mg	2%

BROCCOLI AND CHEESE CHAFFLE

PREP TIME: 5 minutes

COOK TIME: 15 minutes

SERVINGS: 1

Ingredients:

- 1/3 cup broccoli (finely chopped)
- ½ tsp oregano
- 1/8 tsp salt or to taste
- 1/8 tsp ground black pepper or to taste'
- ½ tsp garlic powder
- ½ tsp onion powder
- 1 egg (beaten)
- 4 tbsp shredded cheddar cheese

Directions:

1. Plug the waffle maker to preheat it and spray it with a non-stick cooking spray.
2. In a mixing bowl, combine the cheese, oregano, pepper, garlic, salt and onion. Add the egg and mix until the ingredients are well combined.
3. Fold in the chopped broccoli.
4. Pour an appropriate amount of the batter into your waffle maker and spread out the batter to the edges to cover all the holes on the waffle maker.

5. Close the waffle maker and cook for about 6-8 until the chaffle is browned. Cook time may vary in some waffle makers.

6. After the cooking cycle, use a silicone or plastic utensil to remove the chaffle from the waffle maker.

7. Repeat step 4 to 6 until you have cooked all the batter into chaffles.

8. Serve and top with sour cream as desired.

Nutrition Facts	
Servings: 1	
Amount per serving	
Calories	**198**
% Daily Value*	
Total Fat 13.9g	18%
Saturated Fat 7.3g	37%
Cholesterol 193mg	64%
Sodium 539mg	23%
Total Carbohydrate 5.2g	2%
Dietary Fiber 1.3g	5%
Total Sugars 1.8g	
Protein 13.9g	
Vitamin D 19mcg	94%
Calcium 259mg	20%
Iron 2mg	10%
Potassium 222mg	5%

KETO PROTEIN CHAFFLE

PREP TIME: 5 minutes

COOK TIME: 8 minutes

SERVINGS: 1

Ingredients:

- 1 egg (beaten)
- ½ cup whey protein powder
- A pinch of salt
- 1 tsp baking powder
- 3 tbsp sour cream
- ½ tsp vanilla extract

Topping:

- 2 tbsp heavy cream
- 1 tbsp granulated swerve

Directions:

1. Plug the waffle maker to preheat it and spray it with a non-stick cooking spray.
2. In a mixing bowl, whisk together the egg, vanilla and sour cream.
3. In another mixing bowl, combine the protein powder, baking powder and salt.

4. Pour the flour mixture into the egg mixture and mix until the ingredients are well combined and you form a smooth batter.

5. Pour an appropriate amount of the batter into the waffle maker and spread the batter to the edges to cover all the holes on the waffle maker.

6. Close the waffle maker and cook for about 4 minutes or according to your waffle maker's settings.

7. After the cooking cycle, use a plastic or silicone utensil to remove the chaffle from the waffle iron.

8. Repeat step 4 to 6 until you have cooked all the batter into chaffles.

9. For the topping, whisk together the cream and swerve in a mixing bowl until smooth and fluffy.

10. Top the chaffles with the cream and enjoy.

Nutrition Facts	
Servings: 1	
Amount per serving	
Calories	**445**
% Daily Value*	
Total Fat 25.9g	33%
Saturated Fat 14.4g	72%
Cholesterol 321mg	107%
Sodium 338mg	15%
Total Carbohydrate 13.1g	5%
Dietary Fiber 0.1g	0%
Total Sugars 2.1g	

Nutrition Facts

Servings: 1

Protein 41.6g

Vitamin D 31mcg	155%
Calcium 456mg	35%
Iron 2mg	13%
Potassium 913mg	19%

OKONOMIYAKI CHAFFLE

PREP TIME: 10 minutes

COOK TIME: 8 minutes

SERVINGS: 1

Ingredients:

- 4 tbsp finely shredded cabbage
- 2 eggs (beaten)
- 1/3 cup shredded mozzarella cheese
- 1 slice of bacon (finely chopped)
- A pinch of salt
- 1 tsp tamari sauce
- 1 tbsp chopped green onion
- 1/8 tsp ground black pepper or to taste

Topping:

- 1 tbsp kewpie mayonnaise or American mayonnaise
- 2 tbsp bonito flakes
- 2 tsp Worcestershire sauce

Directions:

1. Heat up a frying pan over medium to high heat and add the chopped bacon.

2. Sear until the bacon is brown and crispy. Use a slotted spoon to transfer the bacon to a paper towel lined plate to drain.

3. Plug the waffle maker to preheat it and spray it with a non-stick spray.

4. In a mixing bowl, combine the crispy bacon, cabbage, cheese, onion, pepper and salt. Add the egg and tamari. Mix until the ingredients are well combined.

5. Pour an appropriate amount of the batter into the waffle maker and spread out the batter to cover all the holes on the waffle maker.

6. Close the waffle maker and cook for about 4 minutes or according to your waffle maker's settings.

7. After the cooking cycle, use a silicone or plastic utensil to remove the chaffle from the waffle maker.

8. Repeat step 5 to 7 until you have cooked all the batter into chaffles.

9. Top the chaffles with sauce, mayonnaise and bonito flakes.

10. Serve warm and enjoy.

Nutrition Facts	
Servings: 1	
Amount per serving	
Calories	**338**
% Daily Value*	
Total Fat 23.3g	30%
Saturated Fat 7.1g	35%
Cholesterol 358mg	119%

Nutrition Facts

Servings: 1

Sodium 1327mg	58%
Total Carbohydrate 9.1g	3%
Dietary Fiber 0.7g	2%
Total Sugars 4.3g	
Protein 22.9g	
Vitamin D 31mcg	154%
Calcium 70mg	5%
Iron 2mg	13%
Potassium 289mg	6%

LEMON CHAFFLE

PREP TIME: 5 minutes

COOK TIME: 12 minutes

SERVINGS: 2

Ingredients:

- 2 tbsp almond flour
- 1 egg
- ½ apple (peeled and finely chopped)
- ½ lemon (juiced)
- ½ tsp lemon zest
- ¼ tsp baking powder
- 2 tsp swerve sweetener
- 2 tbsp cream cheese
- 1/8 tsp salt

Lemon Icing:

- 2 tbsp granulated swerve
- 1 tbsp heavy cream
- ¼ tsp lemon zest
- 1 tsp freshly squeezed lemon juice

Directions:

1. Plug the waffle maker to preheat it and spray it with a non-stick cooking spray.

2. In a mixing bowl, whisk together the egg, lemon zest, cream cheese and lemon juice.

3. In another mixing bowl, combine the salt, swerve, almond flour, baking powder and chopped apple.

4. Pour the egg mixture into the flour mixture and mix until the ingredients are well combined and you have formed a smooth batter.

5. Pour an appropriate amount of the batter into the waffle maker and spread the batter to the edges to cover all the holes on the waffle maker.

6. Close the waffle maker and cook until the chaffle is browned. This will take about 5 minutes; however, the cook time may vary in some waffle maker.

7. After the cooking cycle, use a silicone or plastic utensil to remove the chaffle from the waffle maker.

8. Repeat step 5 to 7 until you have cooked all the batter into chaffles.

9. For the topping, combine the lemon juice, lemon zest, heavy cream and swerve in a mixing bowl. Mix until it is smooth and fluffy.

10. Spread the cream mixture over the chaffles and enjoy.

Nutrition Facts	
Servings: 2	
Amount per serving	
Calories	**174**
% Daily Value*	
Total Fat 12.1g	16%
Saturated Fat 4.9g	24%

Nutrition Facts

Servings: 2

Cholesterol 103mg	34%
Sodium 212mg	9%
Total Carbohydrate 14.2g	5%
Dietary Fiber 2.5g	9%
Total Sugars 7.2g	
Protein 5.5g	
Vitamin D 12mcg	58%
Calcium 71mg	5%
Iron 1mg	7%
Potassium 190mg	4%

BIRTHDAY CAKE CHAFFLE

PREP TIME: 10 minutes

COOK TIME: 12 minutes

SERVINGS: 2

Ingredients:

- 1 egg (beaten)
- 2 tbsp almond flour
- 1 tbsp swerve sweetener
- ½ tsp cake batter extract
- ¼ tsp baking powder
- 1 tbsp heavy whipping cream
- 2 tbsp cream cheese
- ½ tsp vanilla extract
- ½ tsp cinnamon

Frosting:

- 1 tbsp swerve
- ¼ cup heavy whipping cream
- ½ tsp vanilla extract

Directions:

1. Plug the waffle maker to preheat it and spray it with a non-stick spray.

2. In a mixing bowl, combine the cinnamon, almond flour, baking powder and swerve.

3. In another mixing bowl, whisk together the egg, vanilla, heavy cream, and cake batter extract.

4. Pour the flour mixture into the egg mixture and mix until the ingredients are well combined and you have formed a smooth batter.

5. Pour an appropriate amount of the batter into the waffle maker and spread out the waffle maker to cover all the holes on the waffle maker.

6. Close the waffle maker and bake for about 3 minutes or according to your waffle maker's settings.

7. After the cooking cycle, use a silicone or plastic utensil to remove the chaffle from the waffle maker.

8. Repeat step 5 to 7 until you have cooked all the batter into chaffles.

9. For the cream, whisk together the swerve, heavy cream and vanilla extract until smooth and fluffy.

10. To assemble the cake, place one chaffle on a flat surface and spread 1/3 of the cream over it. Layer another chaffle on the first one and spread 1/3 of the cream over it too. Repeat this for the last chaffle and the remaining cream.

11. Cut cake and serve.

Nutrition Facts	
Servings: 2	
Amount per serving	
Calories	249
% Daily Value*	
Total Fat 23.1g	30%

Nutrition Facts
Servings: 2

Saturated Fat 11.8g	59%
Cholesterol 144mg	48%
Sodium 75mg	3%
Total Carbohydrate 6g	2%
Dietary Fiber 1.1g	4%
Total Sugars 0.8g	
Protein 5.8g	
Vitamin D 27mcg	136%
Calcium 92mg	7%
Iron 1mg	5%
Potassium 139mg	3%

SPINACH CHAFFLE

PREP TIME: 5 minutes

COOK TIME: 10 minutes

SERVINGS: 2 chaffles

Ingredients:

- 1 egg (beaten)
- ¼ tsp pepper or to taste
- ½ tsp Italian seasoning
- 1/8 tsp thyme
- ½ cup finely chopped spinach
- ½ cup shredded cheddar cheese
- ¼ cup parmesan cheese for sprinkling

Directions:

1. Plug the waffle maker to preheat it and spray it with a non-stick cooking spray.
2. In a mixing bowl, combine the cheddar, spinach, Italian seasoning, thyme and pepper. Add the egg and mix until the ingredients are well combined.
3. Sprinkle some parmesan cheese over the waffle maker. Pour ½ of the batter into the waffle maker and spread out the batter to cover all the holes on the waffle maker. Sprinkle some cheese over the batter.
4. Close the waffle maker and cook for 5 minutes or according to your waffle maker's settings.

5. After the cooking cycle, use a silicone or plastic utensil to remove the chaffle from the waffle maker.

6. Repeat step 3 to 5 to make the second chaffle.

7. Serve chaffle and top with sour cream or use the chaffles for sandwich.

Nutrition Facts	
Servings: 2	
Amount per serving	
Calories	**192**
% Daily Value*	
Total Fat 14.6g	19%
Saturated Fat 8.5g	42%
Cholesterol 121mg	40%
Sodium 329mg	14%
Total Carbohydrate 1.6g	1%
Dietary Fiber 0.3g	1%
Total Sugars 0.5g	
Protein 14.1g	
Vitamin D 11mcg	55%
Calcium 337mg	26%
Iron 1mg	5%
Potassium 103mg	2%

SHRIMP AVOCADO CHAFFLE SANDWICH

PREP TIME: 10 minutes

COOK TIME: 32 minutes

SERVINGS: 4 sandwiches

Ingredients:

- 2 cups shredded mozzarella cheese
- 4 large eggs
- ½ tsp curry powder
- ½ tsp oregano

Shrimp Sandwich Filling:

- 1-pound raw shrimp (peeled and deveined)
- 1 large avocado (diced)
- 4 slices cooked bacon
- 2 tbsp sour cream
- ½ tsp paprika
- 1 tsp Cajun seasoning
- 1 tbsp olive oil
- ¼ cup onion (finely chopped)
- 1 red bell pepper (diced)

Directions:

1. Plug the waffle maker to preheat it and spray it with a non-stick cooking spray.

2. Break the eggs into a mixing bowl and beat. Add the cheese, oregano and curry. Mix until the ingredients are well combined.

3. Pour an appropriate amount of the batter into the waffle maker and spread out the batter to the edges to cover all the holes on the waffle maker. This should make 8 mini waffles.

4. Close the waffle maker and cook for about 4 minutes or according to your waffle maker's settings.

5. After the cooking cycle, use a silicone or plastic utensil to remove the chaffle from the waffle maker.

6. Repeat step 3 to 5 until you have cooked all the batter into chaffles.

7. Heat up the olive oil in a large skillet over medium to high heat.

8. Add the shrimp and cook until the shrimp is pink and tender.

9. Remove the skillet from heat and use a slotted spoon to transfer the shrimp to a paper towel lined plate to drain for a few minutes.

10. Put the shrimp in a mixing bowl. Add paprika and Cajun seasoning. Toss until the shrimps are all coated with seasoning.

11. To assemble the sandwich, place one chaffle on a flat surface and spread some sour cream over it. Layer some shrimp, onion, avocado, diced pepper and one slice of bacon over it. Cover with another chaffle.

12. Repeat step 10 until you have assembled all the ingredients into sandwiches.

13. Serve and enjoy.

Nutrition Facts	
Servings: 4	
Amount per serving	
Calories	**509**
% Daily Value*	
Total Fat 32.1g	41%
Saturated Fat 9.6g	48%
Cholesterol 456mg	152%
Sodium 891mg	39%
Total Carbohydrate 10.8g	4%
Dietary Fiber 4.2g	15%
Total Sugars 2.5g	
Protein 44.8g	
Vitamin D 18mcg	88%
Calcium 163mg	13%
Iron 2mg	13%
Potassium 698mg	15%

SAVORY PORK RIND CHAFFLE

PREP TIME: 5 minutes

COOK TIME: 10 minutes

SERVINGS: 2

Ingredients:

- ¼ tsp paprika
- ¼ tsp oregano
- ¼ tsp garlic powder
- 1/8 tsp ground black pepper or to taste
- ½ onion (finely chopped)
- ½ cup pork rind (crushed)
- ½ cup mozzarella cheese
- 1 large egg (beaten)

Directions:

1. Plug the waffle maker to preheat it and spray I with a non-stick cooking spray.

2. In a mixing bowl, combine the crushed pork rind, cheese, onion, paprika, garlic powder and pepper. Add the egg and mix until the ingredients are well combined.

3. Pour an appropriate amount of the batter into the waffle maker and spread out the batter to cover all the holes on the waffle maker.

4. Close the waffle maker and cook for about 5 minutes or according to your waffle maker's settings.

5. After the cooking cycle, use a plastic or silicone utensil to remove the chaffle from the waffle maker.

6. Repeat step 3 to 5 until you have cooked all the batter into chaffles.

7. Serve and top with sour cream as desired.

Nutrition Facts	
Servings: 2	
Amount per serving	
Calories	**392**
% Daily Value*	
Total Fat 24g	31%
Saturated Fat 9.6g	48%
Cholesterol 177mg	59%
Sodium 1169mg	51%
Total Carbohydrate 3.6g	1%
Dietary Fiber 0.8g	3%
Total Sugars 1.5g	
Protein 41.9g	
Vitamin D 9mcg	44%
Calcium 29mg	2%
Iron 1mg	4%
Potassium 88mg	2%

LOBSTER CHAFFLE

PREP TIME: 5 minutes

COOK TIME: 8 minutes

SERVINGS: 2

Ingredients:

- 1 egg (beaten)
- ½ cup shredded mozzarella cheese
- ¼ tsp garlic powder
- ¼ tsp onion powder
- 1/8 tsp Italian seasoning

Lobster Filling:

- ½ cup lobster tails (defrosted)
- 1 tbsp mayonnaise
- 1 tsp dried basil
- 1 tsp lemon juice
- 1 tbsp chopped green onion

Directions:

1. Plug the waffle maker to preheat it and spray it with a non-stick cooking spray.
2. In a mixing bowl, combine the mozzarella, Italian seasoning, garlic and onion powder. Add the egg and mix until the ingredients are well combined.

3. Pour an appropriate amount of the batter into the waffle maker and spread out the batter to cover all the holes on the waffle maker.

4. Close the waffle maker and cook for about 4 minutes or according to your waffle maker's settings.

5. After the cooking cycle, use a plastic or silicone utensil to remove and transfer the chaffle to a wire rack to cool.

6. Repeat step 3 to 5 until you have cooked all the batter into chaffles.

7. For the filling, put the lobster tail in a mixing bowl and add the mayonnaise, basil and lemon juice. Toss until the ingredients are well combine.

8. Fill the chaffles with the lobster mixture and garnish with chopped green onion.

9. Serve and enjoy.

Nutrition Facts	
Servings: 2	
Amount per serving	
Calories	117
% Daily Value*	
Total Fat 6.3g	8%
Saturated Fat 1.9g	10%
Cholesterol 141mg	47%
Sodium 303mg	13%
Total Carbohydrate 3g	1%
Dietary Fiber 0.2g	1%
Total Sugars 1g	

Nutrition Facts

Servings: 2

Protein 11.9g

Vitamin D 8mcg	39%
Calcium 57mg	4%
Iron 1mg	3%
Potassium 133mg	3%

SPINACH ARTICHOKE CHAFFLE WITH BACON

PREP TIME: 5 minutes

COOK TIME: 8 minutes

SERVINGS: 2

Ingredients:

- 4 slices of bacon
- ½ cup chopped spinach
- 1/3 cup marinated artichoke (chopped)
- 1 egg
- ¼ tsp garlic powder
- ¼ tsp smoked paprika
- 2 tbsp cream cheese (softened)
- 1/3 cup shredded mozzarella

Directions:

1. Heat up a frying pan and add the bacon slices. Sear until both sides of the bacon slices are browned. Use a slotted spoon to transfer the bacon to a paper towel line plate to drain.

2. Once the bacon slices are cool, chop them into bits and set aside.

3. Plug the waffle maker to preheat it and spray it with a non-stick cooking spray.

4. In a mixing bowl, combine mozzarella, garlic, paprika, cream cheese and egg. Mix until the ingredients are well combined.

5. Add the spinach, artichoke and bacon bit. Mix until they are well incorporated.

6. Pour an appropriate amount of the batter into the waffle maker and spread the batter to the edges to cover all the holes on the waffle maker.

7. Close the waffle maker and cook 4 minutes or more, according to your waffle maker's settings.

8. After the cooking cycle, use a silicone or plastic utensil to remove the chaffle from the waffle maker.

9. Repeat step 6 to 8 until you have cooked all the batter into chaffles.

10. Serve and top with sour cream as desired.

Nutrition Facts	
Servings: 2	
Amount per serving	
Calories	**302**
% Daily Value*	
Total Fat 22.5g	29%
Saturated Fat 8.6g	43%
Cholesterol 137mg	46%
Sodium 998mg	43%
Total Carbohydrate 4.7g	2%
Dietary Fiber 1.8g	6%
Total Sugars 0.6g	

Nutrition Facts	
Servings: 2	
Protein 20.1g	
Vitamin D 8mcg	39%
Calcium 47mg	4%
Iron 2mg	9%
Potassium 408mg	9%

BANANA CHAFFLE

PREP TIME: 5 minutes

COOK TIME: 16 minutes

SERVINGS: 4 chaffles

Ingredients:

- ½ tsp banana flavoring
- 1/8 tsp salt
- 2 tbsp almond flour
- ½ shredded mozzarella cheese
- 2 eggs (beaten)
- ½ tsp baking powder
- ½ tsp cinnamon
- 2 tbsp swerve sweetener

Directions:

1. Plug the waffle maker to preheat it and spray it with a non-stick spray.
2. In a mixing bowl, combine the baking flour, cinnamon, swerve, salt, almond flour and cheese. Add the egg and banana flavor. Mix until the ingredients are well combined.
3. Pour ¼ of the batter into your waffle maker and spread out the batter to cover all the holes on the waffle maker.

4. Close the waffle maker and cook for about 4 minutes or according to your waffle maker's settings.

5. After the cooking cycle, use a silicone or plastic utensil to remove the chaffle from the waffle maker.

6. Repeat step 3 to 5 until you have cooked all the batter into chaffles.

7. Serve warm and enjoy.

Nutrition Facts Servings: 4	
Amount per serving	
Calories	**209**
% Daily Value*	
Total Fat 12.5g	16%
Saturated Fat 3.3g	17%
Cholesterol 93mg	31%
Sodium 171mg	7%
Total Carbohydrate 18.1g	7%
Dietary Fiber 1.7g	6%
Total Sugars 0.7g	
Protein 8.8g	
Vitamin D 8mcg	39%
Calcium 81mg	6%
Iron 1mg	6%
Potassium 94mg	2%

BBQ Chicken Chaffle

PREP TIME: 5 minutes

COOK TIME: 8 minutes

SERVINGS: 2

Ingredients:

- 1 tbsp sugar free BBQ sauce
- 1/3 cup cooked chicken (diced)
- 1 egg (beaten)
- 1 tbsp almond flour
- 1 red bell pepper (chopped)
- ½ cup shredded mozzarella cheese
- ¼ tsp garlic powder
- 1/4 tsp oregano

Directions:

1. Plug the waffle maker to preheat it and spray it with a non-stick cooking spray.
2. In a mixing bowl, whisk together the egg and BBQ sauce. Add the almond flour, mozzarella cheese, pepper, garlic and oregano. Mix until the well combined.
3. Add the diced chicken and mix.
4. Pour and appropriate amount of the batter into the waffle maker and spread the batter to the edges to cover all the holes on the waffle maker.

5. Close the waffle and cook for about 4 minutes.

6. After the cooking cycle, use a silicone or plastic utensil to remove and transfer the chaffle to a wire rack to cool.

7. Repeat step 4 to 6 until you have cooked all the batter into chaffles.

8. Serve warm and enjoy.

Nutrition Facts	
Servings: 2	
Amount per serving	
Calories	**190**
% Daily Value*	
Total Fat 11.3g	15%
Saturated Fat 2.1g	11%
Cholesterol 104mg	35%
Sodium 142mg	6%
Total Carbohydrate 8.8g	3%
Dietary Fiber 2.4g	9%
Total Sugars 3.8g	
Protein 15.2g	
Vitamin D 8mcg	39%
Calcium 58mg	4%
Iron 2mg	8%
Potassium 192mg	4%